EIGHTEENTH CENTURY BIBLIOGRAPHICAL PAMPHLETS
General Editor: JAMES EDWARD TOBIN

JONATHAN SWIFT

A List of Critical Studies
Published from 1895 to 1945

by

LOUIS A. LANDA

and

JAMES EDWARD TOBIN

To Which Is Added

Remarks on Some Swift Manuscripts
in the United States

by

HERBERT DAVIS

OCTAGON BOOKS

A DIVISION OF FARRAR, STRAUS AND GIROUX

New York   1975

Reprinted 1974

by special arrangement with Louis Landa and James Tobin

OCTAGON BOOKS

A Division of Farrar, Straus & Giroux, Inc.

19 Union Square West

New York, N.Y. 10003

Library of Congress Cataloging in Publication Data

Landa, Louis A., 1902-
   Jonathan Swift; a list of critical studies published from 1895
   to 1945.

   Reprint of the ed. published by Cosmopolitan Science and Art
   Service Co., New York, in series: Eighteenth century bibliographical pamphlets.

   1. Swift, Jonathan, 1667-1745—Bibliography. I. Tobin, James
   Edward, 1905-1968, joint author. II. Davis, Herbert John,
   1893-1967. Remarks on some Swift manuscripts in the United
   States. 1974. III. Series: Eighteenth century bibliographical
   pamphlets (New York, 1945-   )

Z8856.L18   1974   016.828′5′09   71-159204
ISBN 0-374-94727-9

Printed in USA by
Thomson-Shore, Inc.
Dexter, Michigan

Preface

The publication of this bibliography coincides with the two-hundredth anniversary of the death of Jonathan Swift. It is highly appropriate that the critical studies of the period covered, 1895 (with a few earlier titles) to 1945, be brought together to commemorate the occasion, for the scholars of the last fifty years have done a particular service in rescuing Swift from the prejudices and misunderstandings of earlier commentators. This is by no means to deny that many vexed problems still remain to be solved; yet the extent of the work that has been done on the canon, on the preparation of accurate texts, and on Swift's life and thought, is imposing in itself and the invaluable basis of future scholarship. And at last it may be said that for the informed scholar the aura of theatricalism which long invested Swift, to the detriment of dispassionate and sensible judgment, has been removed. The formidable number and variety of items comprising this bibliography (615 in all, exclusive of the reviews), need only the obvious comment that they are testimony to the perennial challenge Swift offers to his reader's interest and imagination.

The present pamphlet is the second in a series on eighteenth-century authors and follows in general the procedures of the first (*Alexander Pope*, New York, Cosmopolitan, 1945). The listing of titles in twelve classifications will prove more serviceable, it is hoped, than a single alphabetical arrangement. Overlapping has been avoided wherever possible, but cross references, by item numbers, are intended to direct the reader to similar, supporting, or opposing opinions. The listing of reviews has been kept to a minimum and modern reprintings of Swift's works are mainly restricted to those scholarly editions in which introductory comment, annotations, or textual apparatus are of particular value.

Two further aids are added. An index of 500 names—authors and allusions—supplements the cross referencing of the earlier pages. The editors have also provided some guidance by starring certain titles which effectively present the chief materials, problems, and interpretations of Swift scholarship in the last five decades. This statement is made without prejudice to many of the unstarred titles which, despite their restricted scope and modest pretensions, are often necessary for a full understanding of Swift. It should be particularly observed both that starring has been confined to studies concerned exclusively with Swift, and that it does not necessarily indicate agreement with all or any of the conclusions in the items so distinguished.

The editors are extremely grateful to the officers of The Grolier Club, particularly Mr. George L. McKay and Mr. Edwin De T. Bechtel, for permission to include portions of the 1945 address of President Davis of Smith College before that Society, to Dr. Davis himself for his willingness to allow its publication here, and to the Pierpont Morgan Library for permission to reproduce the only known portrait of Swift which bears his signature.

Louis A. Landa
James E. Tobin

October 19, 1945

Contents

Remarks on Some Swift Manuscripts in the United States

HERBERT DAVIS

SWIFT'S MANUSCRIPTS ARE THE MOST VALUABLE AND intimate memorials that we have of him, pages on which his hand rested as he wrote letters and verses to his friends, volumes from his library marked with pencilled comments often expressing vigorously his private criticism of what he was reading. These memorials are not the less interesting though they reveal him only in his more intimate relationships and show his mind at work in his less formal compositions. We do not possess and we are not likely to discover any of the drafts of *Gulliver's travels* or of *A tale of a tub,* or of his political pamphlets. It was apparently Swift's practice to have a final copy for the printer made by an amanuensis and then to destroy the copy in his own handwriting. There are a few exceptions, however. One MS, from the library of Lord Rothschild, was

[NOTE: These remarks constitute a shortened version of an address by President Herbert Davis of Smith College before the members of The Grolier Club in New York City on November 15, 1945, to commemorate the bicentenary of Swift's death and to open the American exhibition there of Swift books, MSS and memorabilia. Five collections of Swift MSS are referred to in this version, which is presented in the hope that it may supplement the "materials" for the study of the Dean offered in subsequent pages, stimulate increasing interest in his life and work and uncover any Swiftiana that may still be hidden whether uncatalogued in public collections, or unnoticed and neglected in private hands.]

[7]

shown at the recent exhibition in Cambridge, written partly in Swift's hand and partly in the hand of Stella. This was a draft of *The Enquiry into the behaviour of the Queen's last ministry.* There was also a manuscript, with corrections in Swift's autograph, of *An history of the four last years of the Queen,* from the King's Library at Windsor. It is quite possible, also, that a bundle of sermons has survived and may eventually turn up somewhere; but the only MS sermon known at present is that of the sermon on *Brotherly love,* now in the library of Trinity College, Dublin.

Here in America there is only one autograph MS of a prose work. That is the beautiful fair copy, signed and dated, of the *Letter to a very young lady* which may very well be the actual letter sent to Mrs. John Rochfort some ten days after her marriage. It is certainly not the copy which was later sent to the printer when the letter was published in the *Miscellanies, 1727.* The MS is now in the Huntington Library.

The Huntington Library also possesses a fine series of eleven autograph letters to John Barber, Swift's old friend, who became Lord Mayor of London in 1732. The series dates from August 10, 1732 to April 19, 1739, including the greater part of their correspondence printed by Elrington Ball. Swift had seen Barber frequently when he was in London from 1710 to 1714 and had had dealings with him as printer in the city; these letters show how freely Swift turned to his old friends when they were in a position to be useful to him. In spite of his mistake in recommending the unsatisfactory Rev. Matthew Pilkington to be his chaplain, he continued to send his protegés and relatives to Barber for his good offices whenever they went to London.

The rest of the MSS relating to Swift in the Huntington Library originally belonged to Theophilus Swift and were used by Sir Walter Scott in preparing his second edition of Swift's *Works* in 1824. They were sold by Sotheby in July, 1877, to Frederick Locker Sampson, who in turn disposed of them to W. K. Bixby of St. Louis. From Mr. Bixby they came into possession of the Huntington Library.

[NOTE: The exhibition at Cambridge also included Lord Rothschild's copy of an unpublished fragment, in Swift's autograph, of a preface to Sir William Temple's *Works,* "probably a fair copy of a draft which was later discarded"; drafts of *To Charles Ford Esqr. on his birth-day* and *The Bubble,* both printed in Mr. Smith's *Letters of Swift to Ford* (pp. 193, 185); an autograph copy of *The grand question debated,* written three or four years earlier than its publication in 1732; and letters to Addison (Aug. 22, 1710), Bolingbroke (Mar. 1, 1714/15) and Ford (Aug. 14, 1710). Two other items from the Rothschild collection include Swift's annotated copies of Dampier's *A New voyage round the world* (3rd ed., 1698) and Herbert of Cherbury's *The life and raigne of King Henry the Eighth* (1649).]

Some are in the handwriting of Swift. There is a memorandum to Mrs. Whiteway containing directions to be followed in the event of his death, signed, sealed, and witnessed on April 16, 1737. There are examples of trifles in verse and prose exchanged with the Rev. Thomas Sheridan, including *A dialogue in the Hibernian stile.* There is a short draft giving some heads for a pamphlet entitled *Proposal for virtue,* which presumably was never completed; but the character of the piece may be gathered from these final hints:

A contemptuous character of court art, how different from true politicks; for, comparing the talents of two professions that are thought very different, I cannot but think that in the present sense of the word Politician a common sharper and pickpocket has every quality that can be required in the other, and I have personally known more than half a dozen who in their time [were] esteemed equally to excell in both.

The collection also contains some MSS in the handwriting of Sheridan, a very distinctive, legible and modern handwriting which may easily be distinguished from the handwriting of Charles Ford and other friends who copied out many of Swift's verses. Another group of MSS, mainly by younger Irish writers, some endorsed by Swift, was evidently preserved as collected by him, notably the one poem supposed to be written by Stella to the Dean on his birthday and dated November 30, 1721; but the handwriting is certainly not Stella's.

There remains another group of MSS relating to Swift consisting of a few contemporary letters exchanged between Lord Orrery and Mrs. Whiteway, and a few letters from Sir Walter Scott to Mr. James Smith in connection with the loan of these papers for his use.

In the early part of this century some other important collections of MSS were dispersed and found their way to America. A volume of autograph Letters and Poems which had belonged to Sir Andrew Fountaine and remained in possession of the family was sold at Sotheby's on December 5, 1906, and came into Mr. Morgan's possession in 1907. It contains thirty-two items, the most important of which are of course the "MS scraps," autograph copies of four of Swift's early poems: *The story of Baucis and Philemon, The discovery, Vanbrug's house,* and *The history of Vanbrug's house.* These have been used by Mr. Harold Williams in his edition of the *Poems*; and some of the real scraps, such as *A dialogue in the Castilian language,* were published by Mr. Shane Leslie in his *Script of Jonathan Swift.*

The autograph letters of Swift to the Earl of Pembroke, dated June 13, 1709, and to Sir Andrew Fountaine, dated March 6, 1713, and July 30,

[9]

1733, have been included in the *Correspondence* by Elrington Ball; but he printed them from copies in the Forster collection, and there are some slight variants and some misreadings of the original MSS. The collection also includes documents with seals and Swift's signature, and some oddments of verse not in his autograph. There can be no doubt, however, that the unpublished MS of three closely written folio pages, entitled *A modest defense of punning,* is in Swift's own hand. It provides an editor of Swift's works with a curious problem of conscience. For after reading it, he cannot but remember the protests which greeted some of the later volumes added to the collected editions of Swift by his 18th century editors, and the question then raised whether it is fair to add to the canon of a man's work mere trivialities, leisure amusements, or jokes among friends, which have no literary value. Do they complete the picture of the mind of genius, or do they add confusion and distraction unnecessarily?

Apropos of this MS, I must respectfully correct a mistake of the Master of Trinity College, Cambridge, who said, at the exhibition held there to commemorate Swift's death, that he could find no evidence of Swift's connection with Cambridge other than that Gulliver had spent three years at Emmanuel College. Mr. Trevelyan had not seen this MS, dated Cambridge, November 8, 1716, in which Swift replied to the reflections made in a pamphlet called *God's revenge against punning* upon "Divers eminent Clergymen of the University of Cambridge who for having propagated the vice of Punning became great Drunkards and Tories." This Tory dean, a member of Trinity College, Dublin, and of the University of Oxford, came to the defense of the University of Cambridge when it was slandered on November 7, 1716, not by an unknown knight, Sir John Baker, but by the poet, Alexander Pope, because of its fervent loyalty to the Whig cause, for which it had been rewarded by His Majesty with a present of books for its library. Swift ironically defended the University clergymen with this monstrous passage of punning:

For his other Reflection, in calling us Toryes, That much we declare, that His Majesty's *Liberality* in that noble Present of *Books,* as it will make us *Lettered,* so it *Leaves* us *bound* to Him for ever and we should be *covered* with *Gilt,* and deserve to be *bound* as slaves in Turkey, if we failed in our Loyalty; and we hope the *No-Tory*-ety of our Behavior will appear by this further Declaration against all *indefesable Titles* and *Lines* except in His Majesty's *Family* and the *Books* he hath been pleased to give us.

Pope afterwards reprinted *God's revenge against punning,* keeping the pseudonym Sir John Baker, in the last volume of the *Miscellanies 1732,* and we must assume that Swift had never sent him a copy of his reply as he did not include it in the volume. If he had seen it, he might not indeed have liked the flavor of the opening paragraph, for even in this kind of absurd fooling he might think it ill-taste that Swift should attack him as an author ignorant in antiquity, like "a certain gentleman who reading of a *Roman Scholar* thought *Roman* was a *Waterman* and *Scholar* was a *Sculler.*"

There is another volume of manuscripts in the Morgan Library, described as *Autograph Letters of Jonathan Swift to Ford and Others,* which bears the arms of the Earl of Bathurst and came originally from his library. It is the volume from which is taken the unique, unfinished engraver's proof of a portrait of Swift which he has signed himself as if approving it. It is almost certainly engraved after one of the Jervas portraits, probably dating from the time of his visit to Ireland in 1716-17.

The volume also contains the draft of a letter, first published by Mr. Gold in 1937, which was written to Dr. Arbuthnot on July 13, 1714. Swift had addressed a memorial to the Queen dated April 15, 1714, offering to undertake the office of historiographer "not from any view of the profit (which is so inconsiderable, that it will hardly serve to pay the expense of searching offices), but from an earnest desire to serve his queen and country; for which that employment will qualify him, by an opportunity of access to those places where papers and records are kept, which will be necessary to any who undertake such an history." Swift left London on June 1, 1714, travelling to Oxford, and then three days later to Letcombe.

On July 10 Arbuthnot wrote to Swift:

I have talked of your affairs to nobody but my Lady Masham. She tells me, that she has it very much at heart, and would gladly do it for her own sake, and that of her friends; but thinks it not a fit season to speak about it.

To this Swift replied on July 13 and this unsigned autograph seems to be a draft of his letter:

I wonder how you came to mention that Business to Lady M—, if I guess right, that the Business is the Histor—'s Place; it is in the D. of Shr—s Gift, and he sent Ld Bol— word that tho he was under some Engagem—, he would give it me So, since which time I never mentioned it, tho I had a memorial some months in my Pocket, which I believe you saw, but I would never give it to Lady M— because things were embroyld with her I would not give two Pence to have it for the Value of it; but I had been told by Ld B. Lady M— and you, that the Qu— had a Concern for her History &c: & I was ready to undertake it. I thought Ld Bol— would have done such a Trifle, but I shall not concern myself, and I should be sorry the Qu— should be asked for it otherwise than as what would be for her Honor and Reputation with Posterity &c. Pray how long do you think I should be suffered to hold that Post in the next Reign. I have inclosed you the originall Memorial as I intended it; and if Ld Bol— thinks it of any moment, let him do it: but do not

[11]

give him the Memorial, unless he be perfectly willing: For I insist again upon it, that I am not asking a Favor: and there is an End of that Matter, only one word more, that I would not accept it if offered, only that it would give me an Opportunity of seeing those I esteem and love, the little time that they will be in Power. You desire me to come to Town, indeed I will not: I am overcoming you by Absence as fast as I can, and you would have me come and break my Heart. Shall I not be miserable to stand by and see things going every day nearer to ruin; can I (as I have repeated to you often) do the least good to my self, my Friends, or the Publick: and do you think I have not too much Spirit to continue where I have no Call, and be wholly insignificant. . . .

But as a matter of general interest there is nothing that can compare with the five autograph letters to Charles Ford and other documents composed by Swift but not in his hand, all connected with arrangements for the publication of *Gulliver's Travels*—both when it first appeared in 1726 and again when Swift was concerned with its revision for the corrected edition in 1727, and for the Dublin edition which appeared in 1735. Here, for instance, is the original offer to Mr. Benjamin Motte, the printer, in a letter dated August 8, 1726, from Richard Sympson, Gulliver's cousin, making the strange proposal to him to read the manuscript and "within three days deliver a Bank Bill of two hundred pounds, wrapt up so as to make a parcel to the Hand from whence you receive this, who will come in the same manner exactly at 9 o'clock at night on Thursday which will be the 11th Instant," and the autograph of Motte's reply. There is a small half-sheet with three lines signed in the same way, giving further instructions on August 13th: "I would have both volumes come out together and published by Christmas at furthest." The next spring, April 27, 1727, Richard Sympson, in an entirely different handwriting, sends another note to Mr. Motte, giving full power to Erasmus Lewis, Esq. to treat with him concerning his Cousin Gulliver's book, together with Lewis' receipt to Motte "I am fully satisfyd," dated May 4, 1727. Also among the five letters to Charles Ford which were first printed by Mr. Nichol Smith in 1935 is the important letter, dated November 20, 1733, about the Irish edition of *Gulliver*. Swift's statement is a very emphatic endorsement of his concern with the Dublin edition printed by Faulkner.

I gave you an account in my last how against my will a Man here is printing the Works of &c by Subscription. Gulliver vexeth me more than any. I thought you had entred in leaves interlined all the differences from the originall Manuscript. Had there been onely omissions, I should not care one farthing; but change of Style, new things foysted in, that are false facts, and I know not what, is very provoking. Motte tells me He designs to print a new Edition of Gulliver in quarto, with Cutts and all as it was in the genuin copy. He is very uneasy about the Irish Edition. All I can do is to strike out the Trash in the Edition to be printed here, since you can not help me. I will order your name, as you desire, among the Subscribers. It was to avoyd offence, that Motte got those alterations and insertions

[12]

to be made I suppose by Mr. Took the Clergyman deceased. So that I fear the second Edition will not mend the matter, further than as to litteral faults. For instance, The Title of one Chapter is of the Queens administration without a prime Minister &c, and accordingly in the Chapter it is said that she had no chief Minister &c: Besides, the whole Sting is taken out in severall passages, in order to soften them. Thus the Style is debased, the humor quite lost, and the matter insipid.

The interleaved copy of *Gulliver's Travels* showing all the differences from the original manuscript is now in the Morgan Library, and a careful examination of the printed text and of these interleaved pages shows the reason for Swift's concern. They prove also that Swift was not content with the corrected London edition, and that Faulkner's text, printed in 1735, may be regarded as having his final approval.

Another MS in the handwriting of Charles Ford is a fair copy made on three small sheets of the delightful verses called *Stella at Wood Park*. This MS is bound up with another copy of the same poem with variant readings, written on two sides of a foolscap sheet badly discolored and in places hardly legible. It is described by Mr. Shane Leslie as Swift's original manuscript. This can hardly be true, as it is evidently a later copy, with curious varieties of spelling, of the version copied by Ford. It is unlike Ford's handwriting, but in my opinion it is also unlike any writing of Swift that I have seen early or late.

There can be no doubt whatever about the handsome MS recently acquired by the Morgan Library of Swift's poem entitled *Apollo to the Dean*. It is a fair copy on three large sheets in the Dean's hand with four lines deleted on the second page which were afterwards elaborated and replaced by a passage of twenty-four lines. It must therefore be an early version of the poem.

There is one other volume of MSS in the Morgan Library described as "the Earl of Orrery's collection, comprising a very fine and extensive series of autograph letters of Dean Swift to the Earl." The volume was sold at Sotheby's in 1906 and acquired by the Morgan Library in 1907. There is certainly no doubt that the letters come from Lord Orrery's collection; they are so carefully arranged, numbered and endorsed by His Lordship: the first, dated March 22, 1732, "in answer to a letter received from me," the second, "concerning the verses I sent to him on his birthday," and the last, number twenty, dated November 21, 1738, with the note added "his illness hindered him writing to me afterwards." The volume also contains some small engravings and affidavits connected with Dr. Wilson's attack on Swift, and a copy of those Memoirs written by Swift as notes for an account of his own life.

[13]

The rest of the Orrery Papers are a very large collection of many items, MSS in the hands of Orrery and Lady Orrery, together with annotated and interleaved copies of his own printed works now in the library of Harvard University. Some of these volumes seem to have been prepared in Orrery's careful and methodical way, certainly as a complete record of his correspondence, if not for publication, with title, marginal notes, and index in his own handwriting. Others are copies made by his secretary in Ireland and covering only the periods when he was in residence there. The third volume is of particular importance in connection with Swift as it contains a number of copies of his poems, together with passages omitted from the printed versions both in prose and in verse.

In the Harvard collection there are autograph MSS of two letters, one a letter to Mrs. Pratt, thanking her for the gift of a screen which she had sent from England in the spring of 1725. It was a firescreen adorned with painted maps and may be taken as an indication that Swift's Dublin friends were fully aware of his preoccupation with travel at this time. The other is the autograph of a letter to Charles Ford, dated October 9, 1733, and included in Mr. Nichol Smith's edition of the Letters to Ford.

Harvard also possesses three volumes which were in Swift's possession. The first is Thomas Herbert's *A relation of some yeares travaile, begunne Anno. 1626 into Afrique and greater Asia &c.* (London, 1634). On the flyleaf is the date 1720, Swift's signature, and this comment: "If this booke were stript of its Impertinence, Conceitedness and tedious Digressions, it would be almost worth reading and would then be two thirds smaller than it is." The second is a copy of *The club, etc.* by James Puckle, 1713, which also contains the signature of Pope on the title page. Special passages are noted in the margin with a pencilled mark, representing the fingers of a hand which I have found in some of Swift's own books. And it would be like him to notice proverbs, even such a moral one as the Turkish proverb quoted in the character of the drunkard: "There's a devil in every grape." He may well have added also the mark in the margin drawing attention to one of the rare projects of the projector, namely, "To save Waterman the labour of rowing against Tide, he had contriv'd to make the Thames continually to ebb on one side, and flow on t'other." The third is the Dublin edition (1736) of a Latin play by Mr. Ruggle of Clare Hall, which had been acted before the Earl of Oxford in 1713. It carries also the signature of Edw. Synge, and therefore may have been given to him by Swift. He was the son of the Archbishop and, as Chancellor of St. Patrick's, had been Swift's adviser on musical matters.

[14]

The collection at Yale Library, which contains an unusually fine group of early editions, especially of the *Drapier Letters,* has also a handsome folio from Swift's library, Bodin's *Les six livres de la republique,* (Paris, 1576), with the signature Jon. Swift 1709, and on the inner side of the cover an autograph note, signed Jonath Swift, April 2, 1725:

This Author was a Man of very great Reading, he excells in setting the Arguments on both sides of a Question in the strongest Light: but often (in my Judgment) decides wrong. He handles Government too much like a Lawyer, and grossly mistakes that of England. He shews some Inconveniences in Aristocracyes and Democracyes as necessary, which are easily avoydable. He seems not to have considered the Nature of representing many by few. His Royall Monarchy, which he proposeth as the most Perfect Government is visionary, unless every Country were sure to have always a good King, for he leaves the absolute Power of making and annulling Laws in the Will of the Soverain, although a single Person, contrary to the Judgment of the wisest Writers upon Government. His whimsicall Discourses upon Astrology and the Influence of the Starrs upon human Nature, together with his Digressions upon the Power of Numbers and Harmony are not I think to be otherwise accounted for than by some odd Turn in the Author's Brain, or a Vanity to shew his Acquaintance with Sciences out of his Way.

There are also a number of pencilled comments in the margins which show how carefully Swift read the book and with what contempt he rejected some of its arguments. These jottings vary from slight corrections to remarks such as *mal raisonne par tout, l'ignorant,* or when Bodin becomes too extravagant in his adoration of the grand Monarch as the image of the living God, simply *le coquin, le sot.*

It has been several times suggested to me that Swift's political arguments concerning the relationship of Ireland to England were useful for American writers at the time of the struggle for independence; but these arguments were available in other and earlier sources. I was therefore much interested to find among the Johnson Family Papers at Yale a letter from William Livingston, who later became Governor of New Jersey, to Noah Wells at Yale, dated May 27, 1742, commenting with much enthusiasm on Swift's satire of the King and the Prince of Wales, and enclosing a MS copy of his *Rhapsody on poetry.* "It is so rare a book," he says, "that but two of them ever came to this province, being in great measure prevented by Walpole against whom the plan of the poem is levelled, mine also being in manuscript."

There must be MSS or annotated volumes still unnoticed in unexpected places, such as the MS letter belonging to the Philadelphia Historical Society. Written to Mr. Pulteney, dated Dublin, March 8, 1736, it is a MS copy of Swift's letter which was printed by Elrington Ball from an autograph draft in the British Museum, dated March 7, 1736-7. It is worth comparing the two versions, for it seems probable that Swift's secretary has tried to improve the original draft, smoothing out some of its rough transitions and toning down its violence by changes and omissions. For instance the formal copy reads:

I desire that my Prescriptions for Health, which you intend to follow, may be made publick for the benefit of Mankind, although I very much dislike the Animal as it hath acted for severall Years past, nor ever valued myself as a Philanthropus.

Swift's draft of this passage was rather stronger:

I desire that my prescription of living may be published, which you design to follow, for the benefit of mankind; which, however, I do not value a rush, nor the animal itself, as it now acts, neither will I ever value myself as a Philanthropus, because it is now a creature, taking a vast majority, that I hate more than a toad, a viper, a wasp, a stork, a fox, or any other that you will please to add.

Critical Studies: 1895 to 1945

ABBREVIATIONS

ELH — *Journal of English literary history*

ESt — *Englische Studien*

HLQ — *Huntington library quarterly*

JEGP — *Journal of English and Germanic philology*

JHI — *Journal of the history of ideas*

MLN — *Modern language notes*

MLQ — *Modern language quarterly*

MLR — *Modern language review*

MP — *Modern philology*

N&Q — *Notes and queries*

PMLA — *Publications of the Modern language association*

PQ — *Philological quarterly*

RAA — *Revue Anglo-américaine*

RES — *Review of English studies*

RLC — *Revue de la littérature comparée*

SP — *Studies in philology*

SRL — *Saturday review of literature*

TLS — *London Times literary supplement*

I. BIBLIOGRAPHY

1. Barnett, George L.: "Gay, Swift, and Tristram Shandy" [on a poem attributed to Swift], *N&Q*, 185 (Dec. 4, 1943), 346-47.
2. Beattie, Lester M.: "The authorship of the Quidnuncki's" [attributed to Arbuthnot, not Swift], *MP*, 30 (Feb. 1933), 317-20.
3. Boys, Richard C.: "A finding list of English poetical miscellanies 1700-1748 in selected American libraries," *ELH*, 7 (June 1940), 144-62. Addenda to 4.
4. Case, Arthur E.: *A bibliography of English poetical miscellanies 1521-1750*, Oxford, for the Bibliographical society, 1935 [for 1929].
4a. *Catalogue of the exhibition held in the library of Trinity College, Dublin, from October 19 to November 23, 1945, to commemorate the bicentenary of the death of Jonathan Swift*, Dublin, Friends of the Library, 1945.
5. Cornu, Donald: "Swift, Motte, and the copyright struggle: two unnoticed documents," *MLN*, 54 (Feb. 1939), 114-24.
6. *Davis, Herbert: "The canon of Swift," in *English institute annual, 1942*, New York, Columbia U.P., 1943, pp. 119-36.
7. Dennis, G. R.: "Gulliver's travels" [large paper edition, with handwriting of Charles Ford], *Athenaeum*, 111, no. 3666 (Jan. 29, 1898), 153-54. See G. A. Aitken, *ibid.*, no. 3668 (Feb. 12, 1898), 215-16.
8. Dobell, Percy J.: *A catalogue of works by Dr. Jonathan Swift, together with contemporary works relating to or illustrative of the life and works of the Dean of St. Patrick's, Dublin*, London, Dobell [1933. Catalogue no. 105].
9. Firth, Sir Charles H.: "The canon of Swift" [*Jack Frenchman's lamentation*], *RES*, 3 (Jan. 1927), 73-74. Comment on 29.
10. Griffith, Reginald Harvey: *Alexander Pope: a bibliography*, Austin, U. of Texas, 1922-27, 2 pts. in 3 v.
11. Grose, Clyde Leclare: *A select bibliography of British history, 1660-1760*, Chicago, U. of Chicago Press [1939], pp. 352-55.
12. "Gulliver's travels" [bibliographical problems], *TLS*, Nov. 11, 1926, p. 804.

12a. [Hayward, John:] *A catalogue of printed books and manuscripts, by Jonathan Swift, D.D. Exhibited in the Old Schools in the University of Cambridge. To commemorate the 200th anniversary of his death,* Cambridge, Cambridge U.P., 1945. (Drawn chiefly from the Rothschild and Williams collections). See summary by H. Williams, *TLS,* Oct. 20, 1945, p. 504.

13. *Hubbard, L. L.: *Contributions towards a bibliography of Gulliver's travels to establish the number and order of issue of the Motte editions of 1726 and 1727,* Chicago, W. Hill, 1922. See 30; 32.

14. *Jackson, W. Spencer: "Bibliography of Swift's works," in *Prose works of Jonathan Swift,* ed. by Temple Scott, London, Bell, 1908, v. 12, pp. 109-241. See 21; 26.

15. Kirkpatrick, T. Percy C.: "Faulkner's edition of Swift" [and former's letter of 1744], *TLS,* Apr. 12, 1934, p. 262. See 449.

16. *Mayo, Thomas F.: "The authorship of *The history of John Bull,*" *PMLA,* 45 (Mar. 1930), 274-82. Refutation of 466.

17. Morgan, William Thomas, and Morgan, Chloe Siner: *A bibliography of British history (1700-1715), with special reference to the reign of Queen Anne,* Bloomington, U. of Indiana, 1939, v. 3, pp. 139-43; 251-58 [*The Examiner*]. See also v. 5 (1942), pp. 445-46.

18. "The poems of Swift. Establishing the canon," *TLS,* Aug. 21, 1937, pp. 597-98.

19. "Private libraries. IV—Lord Rothschild," *TLS,* Aug. 6, 1938, p. 524.

20. "Private libraries. V—Harold Williams," *TLS,* Aug. 27, 1938, p. 560.

21. *Teerink, H.: *A bibliography of the writings in prose and verse of Jonathan Swift, D.D.,* The Hague, Nijhoff, 1937. See H. Williams, *RES,* 13 (July 1937), 366-72; Lord Rothschild, *Library,* 4th ser., 18 (Sept. 1937), 224-28; *TLS,* Mar. 20, 1938, p. 228; R. K. Root, *PQ,* 17 (Apr. 1938), 207-8.

22. Thompson, Paul Vern: "The canon of Swift, 1674-1714," in *Summaries of doctoral dissertations, Northwestern University,* 5 (1937), 29-33.

23. ——: "The canon of Swift" [on the authorship of *Tripos*], *RES,* 14 (Apr. 1938), 182-89. See H. Williams, *ibid.* (July 1938), 326-27.

24. Tobin, James E.: *Eighteenth century English literature and its cultural background: a bibliography,* New York, Fordham U.P., 1939.

[20]

25. [Wagner, Henry R.:] *Irish economics 1700-1783: a bibliography with notes,* London, J. Davy, 1907. [Collection now at Yale Univ.].

26. White, Newport B.: "Bibliography of Dean Swift," *TLS,* June 9, 1927, p. 408. Addenda to 14.

27. ——: "Swiftiana in Marsh's library," *Hermathena,* 11 (1901), 369-81. Reprinted in *An account of Archbishop Marsh's library,* Dublin, Hodges, 1926, pp. 20-30.

28. Wiley, Autrey Nell: *Jonathan Swift, 1667-1745. An exhibition of printed books at the University of Texas, October 19 - December 31, 1945,* Austin, Univ. of Texas [Library: Rare book collections], 1945.

29. Williams, Harold: "The canon of Swift" [*Jack Frenchman's lamentation*], *RES,* 2 (July 1926), 322-28; 3 (Apr. 1927), 212-14. See 9.

30. *——: *"Gulliver's travels*: further notes," *Library,* 4th ser., 9 (Sept. 1928), 187-96. Addenda to 32.

31. *——: "Jonathan Swift," *Cambridge bibliography of English literature,* ed. by F. W. Bateson, Cambridge U.P., and New York, Macmillan, 1941, v. 2, pp. 581-96.

32. *——: "The Motte editions of *Gulliver's travels,*" *Library,* 4th ser., 6 (Dec. 1925), 229-63. See 30.

33. ——: "Swift: Miscellanies in prose and verse. Second ed. 1713," *Bibliographical notes and queries,* 2, xi (Nov. 1938), 10.

See also: 330, 339, 359, 449, 457, 468, 470, 505, 510, 527, 551, 561.

II. BIOGRAPHY

34. Ainger, Alfred: "Swift—his life and genius," in *Lectures and essays,* London, Macmillan, 1905, v. 1, pp. 188-272.

35. Allen, Robert J.: *The clubs of Augustan London,* Cambridge, Harvard U.P., 1933.

36. Alton, E. H.: "Some fragments of college history" [Swift and P. Delany], *Hermathena,* nos. 57-58 (May, Nov., 1941), 25-38, 121-65.

37. *Babcock, R. W.: "Swift's conversion to the Tory party," in *Univ. of Michigan publications in language and literature (Essays and Studies in English and comparative literature*), 8 (1932), 133-49.

[21]

38. Ball, F. Elrington: "Swift at Havisham" [i.e. Harrietsham, with Richard Coleire], *N&Q*, 12th ser., 7 (Oct. 30, 1920), 353.

39. Barrington, E.: "The mystery of Stella," *Atlantic monthly*, 129 (Mar. 1922), 311-23. [Fictionalized biography].

40. Barry, W. F.: "A fresh view of Dean Swift," *Contemporary review*, 69 (May 1896), 644-57.

41. Beattie, Lester M.: *John Arbuthnot, mathematician and satirist*, Cambridge, Harvard U.P., 1935. See 16; 466.

42. Bell, Mrs. Hugh [Lady Florence Eveleen Eleanore Oliffe]: *The dean of St. Patrick's: a play in four acts*, London, Arnold, 1903.

43. Bensly, Edward: "The library at Moor park," *N&Q*, 159 (July 19, 1930), 48.

44. —— and Strachan, L. R. M.: "The broken Cremona," *N&Q*, 168 (Jan. 12, 1935), 34.

45. ——: "Swift's Welsh travels," *N&Q*, 146 (Mar. 29, 1924), 238-39.

46. Bernard, John Henry: *The cathedral church of St. Patrick . . . with a short account of the deans*, rev. by J. E. L. Oulton, Dublin and Cork, Talbot, 1940.

47. ——: "Dean Swift in Dublin," *Blackwood's magazine*, 180 (Nov. 1906), 676-93.

48. *——: "The relations between Swift and Stella," in *Prose works of Jonathan Swift*, ed. by T. Scott, London, Bell, 1908, v. 12, pp. 85-106. See 72.

49. Birrell, Augustine: "Dean Swift," in *Collected essays and addresses, 1880-1920*, London and Toronto, Dent, 1922, v. 1, pp. 86-93.

50. Birss, John H.: "A volume from Swift's library," *N&Q*, 163 (Dec. 3, 1932), 404 [Anne Killigrew's *Poems*]; 164 (May 13, 1933), 334 [Molesworth's *Account of Denmark*]; 166 (Apr. 28, 1934), 295 [*Vertu du Catholicon, 1612*]. Addenda to 182.

51. Boyling, P. J.: "Decay of hating," *London quarterly and Holborn review*, 163 (Jan. 1938), 80-84. Review of 145.

52. Brawner, J. P.: "Swift and the Harley-St. John ministry," in *West Virginia Univ. Philological studies*, 3 (1939), 46-59.

53. Brégy, Katherine: "The enigma of Dean Swift," *Catholic world*, 112 (Oct. 1920), 52-59.

54. Brooks, E. St. John: "Swift and Dr. [Francis] Wilson," *TLS*, Aug. 7, Oct. 9, 1943, pp. 379, 487. Comment on 87.

55. Cabanès, Auguste: "Swift," in *Grandes neuropathes*, Paris, Michel [1935], v. 3.

56. *Case, Arthur E.: "Swift and Sir William Temple—a conjecture" [early life and deafness], *MLN,* 60 (Apr. 1945), 259-65. See 185.

57. Challemel-Lacour, P. A.: *Etudes et réflexions d'un pessimiste,* Paris, Bibliothèque-Charpentier, 1901, pp. 128-39.

58. Clewes, Winston: *The violent friends,* London, Michael Joseph, 1944; also New York, Appleton-Century, 1945. [Fiction].

59. Collins, A. S.: *Authorship in the days of Johnson. Being a study of the relation between author, patron, publisher and public, 1726-1780,* London, Holden, 1927.

60. Collins, John Churton: *Jonathan Swift, a biographical and critical study* [1893], London, Chatto & Windus, 1902.

61. Colum, Padraic: "At Swift's rectory," *Bookman* [New York], 70 (Sept. 1929), 39-42.

62. Corde, Eleanor: *Dean Swift, a drama,* Los Angeles, McBride, 1922.

63. Corkery, Daniel: "Ourselves and Dean Swift," *Studies,* 23 (June 1934), 203-18. Comment on 92; 156; 267.

64. "The counting habit and Dean Swift," *Spectator,* 124 (Apr. 3, 1920), 449-50.

65. Cowie, A.: "Shackled satirist," *SRL,* 23 (Jan. 4, 1941), 13. Review of 90.

66. *Craik, Sir Henry: *The life of Jonathan Swift* [1882], London, Murray, 1894, 2v.

67. Crawley, W. J. Chetwoode, and Kenning, George: "Early Irish freemasonry and Dean Swift's connection with the craft," in *Masonic reprints and historical revelations,* by H. Sadler, London, 1898.

68. Dark, Sidney: "Jonathan Swift," in *Five deans,* London, Cape [1928]; also New York, Harcourt, 1928, pp. 109-53.

69. Darnall, F. M.: "Swift's belief in immortality," *MLN,* 47 (Nov. 1932), 448-51.

70. ——: "Traditional notions about Jonathan Swift," *English journal,* 14 (Sept. 1925), 514-21.

71. ——: "Was Swift ambitious?" *English journal,* 21 (Nov. 1932), 733-42.

72. *Davis, Herbert: *Stella: a gentlewoman of the eighteenth century,* New York, Macmillan, 1942. See L. A. Landa, *PQ,* 22 (Apr. 1943), 176-77; R. Quintana, *U. of Toronto quarterly,* 12 (July 1943), 508-11.

73. de Castro, J. Paul: "Swift and Mrs. Oldfield" [in 1713], *N&Q,* 12th ser., 5 (Sept. 1919), 230-31.

74. de Castro, J. Paul: "Swift and Walpole" [request for deanery of Wells, 1713], *N&Q*, 12th ser., 5 (Oct. 1919), 262-63.

75. Dickins, Lilian, and Stanton, Mary: *An eighteenth century correspondence, being the letters of Deane Swift, . . .* London, Murray, 1910.

76. Dobrée, Bonamy: *William Congreve: a conversation between Swift and Gay*, Seattle, U. of Washington bookstore, 1929. Reprinted in *As their friends saw them*, London, Cape, 1933, pp. 75-92.

77. Duff, I. F. Grant: "A one-sided sketch of Jonathan Swift," *Psychoanalytic quarterly*, 6 (Apr. 1937), 238-59.

78. Elgar, Edward: "Swift in Bury St.," *TLS*, Aug. 10, 1922, p. 521.

79. Escott, T. H. S.: "Jonathan Swift in pulpit and press," *London quarterly review*, 114 (July 1910), 39-57.

80. Falkiner, Sir Frederick: *The foundation of the Hospital and free school of King Charles II, Oxmantown*, Dublin, Sealy, 1906.

81. *——: "On the portraits, busts, and engravings of Swift, and . . . Stella," in *Prose works of Jonathan Swift*, ed. by T. Scott, London, Bell, 1908, v. 12, pp. 1-82. See 159.

82. Feiling, Keith: *History of the Tory party, 1640-1714*, Oxford, Clarendon, 1924.

83. *Firth, Sir Charles: "Dean Swift and ecclesiastical preferment," *RES*, 2 (Jan. 1926), 1-17.

84. *Forster, John: *The life of Jonathan Swift, Vol. I, 1667-1711*, London, Murray, 1875. [No more published].

85. Gibbs, Lewis [pseud. for Joseph W. Cove]: *Vanessa and the Dean: the ironic history of Esther Vanhomrigh and Jonathan Swift*, London, Dent, 1938; also New York, Funk & Wagnalls, 1939. [Fiction].

86. Gloor, Gertrud: *Swift und die Frauen*, Freising-München, Datterer, 1922. See 139.

87. Gold, Maxwell B.: "The Brennan affidavit," *TLS*, May 17, 1934, p. 360. See H. Williams, *ibid.*, May 24, 1934, p. 376; *T.L.S.*, *ibid.*, Aug. 21, 1943, p. 403; and 54.

88. ——: "Swift's admission to Mrs. Whiteway confirmed," *PMLA*, 49 (Sept. 1934), 964-65. See 112.

89. *——: *Swift's marriage to Stella, together with unprinted and misprinted letters*, Cambridge, Harvard U.P., 1937. See H. Davis, *MP*, 34 (May 1937), 434-35; E. Pons, *Etudes Anglaises*, 1 (Nov. 1937), 537-40; H. Williams, *RES*, 14 (Jan. 1938), 108-10; R. K. Root, *PQ*, 17 (Apr. 1938), 205-6; and 72; 116.

90. Goodwin, Frank Stier: *Jonathan Swift, giant in chains,* New York, Liveright, 1940. See 65.

91. Gregory, Alyse: "Stella, Vanessa and Swift," *Nineteenth century,* 113 (June 1933), 755-64.

92. Gwynn, Stephen: *The life and friendships of Dean Swift,* London, Butterworth, 1933; also New York, Holt, 1933. See W. A. Eddy, *SP,* 31 (July 1934), 490-95; J. M. Purcell, *PQ,* 13 (July 1934), 316-17; F. T. Wood, *ESt,* 69 (July 1934), 117-19; and 63; 211.

93. ———: "A manuscript assigned to Swift" [commonplace book of political verse], *Athenaeum,* 108, no. 3605 (Nov. 28, 1896), 759. See A. F. Robbins, *ibid.,* no. 3607 (Dec. 12, 1896), 838.

94. Hamilton, G. F.: "Dean Swift as a churchman," *Irish church quarterly,* July 1917.

95. Hand, George: "Swift and marriage," in *Essays and studies by members of the department of English* (Univ. of California Publications in English, 14), Berkeley, 1943, pp. 73-93. See 72.

96. Hassall, Arthur: *Life of Lord Bolingbroke,* Oxford, Blackwell, 1915.

97. Hearsey, Marguerite: "New light on the evidence for Swift's marriage," *PMLA,* 42 (Mar. 1927), 157-61.

98. Heidenhain, Adolf: *Ueber den Menschenhass: eine pathographische Untersuchung ueber Jonathan Swift,* Stuttgart, Enke, 1934. See M. A. Korn, *ESt,* 69 (July 1934), 120-24.

99. Higgins, T. F.: "Swiftiana" [references to Swift in contemporary Dublin journals], *TLS,* Aug. 30, Dec. 13, 1934, pp. 589, 895.

100. Hinchman, W. S., and Gummere, F. B.: "Jonathan Swift," in *Lives of great English writers,* Boston, Houghton, 1908, pp. 154-73.

101. Hone, Joseph M.: "Ireland and Swift," *Dublin magazine,* 8 (July-Sept. 1933), pp. 9-17.

102. Howes, Raymond F.: "Jonathan Swift and the conversation of the coffee houses," *Quarterly journal of speech,* 17 (Feb. 1931), 14-24.

103. Hutton, William H.: *The English church from the accession of Charles I to the death of Queen Anne,* London, Macmillan, 1903.

104. Huxley, Aldous: "Swift," in *Do what you will,* London, Chatto, 1929, pp. 93-106; also New York, Doubleday, 1929, pp. 99-112.

105. Irving, William Henry: *John Gay: favorite of the wits,* Durham, Duke U.P., 1940.

106. Isaacs, J., ed.: *Memoirs of Mrs. Letitia Pilkington, 1712-1750,* intro. by Iris Barry, London, Routledge, 1928.

[25]

107. Jackson, Robert Wyse: "Dean Swift's tour of Munster," *Dublin magazine*, 18 (Apr.-June 1943), 33-39.

108. *——: *Jonathan Swift, dean and pastor,* London, Society for the propagation of Christian knowledge, 1939.

109. ——: "Sidelights on Swift," *Dublin magazine*, 17 (Jan.-Mar. 1942), 47-55; (Apr.-June 1942), 32-36.

109a. ——: *Swift and his circle. A book of essays, with a foreword by Seumas O'Sullivan,* Dublin, Talbot, 1945. See 236a.

110. Jacobson, A. C.: "Literary genius and manic-depressive insanity with special reference to the alleged case of Dean Swift," *Scientific American,* Supplement, 75 (Jan. 4, 1913), 2. Takes issue with 152.

111. Jebb, Richard C.: *Bentley* [1882], New York, Harper, 1902.

112. Johnston, Denis: "The mysterious origin of Dean Swift," *Dublin historical record,* 3 (1941), 81-97. Refuted by H. Williams, *TLS,* Nov. 29, 1941, p. 596; see also "Swift's secret," *ibid.,* Sept. 13, 1941, p. 459; W. S. Kerr, *ibid.,* Oct. 4, 1941, p. 495; and 88; 184.

113. Jourdan, G. V.: "The religion of Jonathan Swift," *Church quarterly review,* 126 (July 1938), 269-86.

114. King, Richard Ashe: *Swift in Ireland,* London, Unwin, 1895.

115. King, William: "Dean Swift's library," *Book collector's quarterly,* 4, no. 13 (Jan.-Mar. 1934), 76-80. Comment on 182.

116. Kirkpatrick, T. Percy C.: "Swift and Stella," *TLS,* June 19, 1937, p. 464. Comment on 89.

117. *Landa, Louis A.: "Swift and charity," *JEGP,* 44 (Oct. 1945), 337-50.

118. Lane-Poole, Stanley: "The alleged marriage of Swift and Stella," *Fortnightly review,* 93 (Feb. 1910), 319-32.

119. Law, R. K.: "On the death of Stella," *Spectator,* 140 (Jan. 28, 1928), 108-9.

120. Lawlor, Hugh Jackson: "The deaneries of St. Patrick's," *Journal of the Royal society of antiquaries of Ireland,* 62 (1932), 103-13.

121. ——: *The fasti of St. Patrick's, Dublin,* Dundalk, Tempest, 1930.

122. ——: "The graves of Swift and Stella," *English historical review,* 33 (Jan. 1918), 89-93.

123. Lawrence, G. E.: *Swift and Stella: a play,* London, Gowans, 1928.

124. *Le Fanu, T. P.: "Catalogue of Dean Swift's library in 1715, with an inventory of his personal property in 1742," *Proceedings of the Royal Irish academy,* 37 (July 1927), 263-75.

125. Le Fanu, T. P: "Dean Swift's library," *Journal of the Royal society of antiquaries of Ireland,* 26 (1896), 113-21. See 182.

126. Legg, J. Wickham:"Swift and his giddiness," *TLS,* Nov. 21, 1918, p. 569. See *The academy,* 19 (June 1881), 475; 24 (July 1883), 64; also replies by H. Craik, C. Mercier, and D. Guthrie, *TLS,* Nov. 28, 1918, p. 583.

127. Lennox, Patrick J.: "Swift, the Irish patriot," *Catholic educational review,* 14 (1917), 289-99.

128. Leslie, Shane: "Dean Swift and Vanessa," *Bookman* [New York], 66 (Feb. 1928), 628-34.

129. *——: *The script of Jonathan Swift and other essays,* Philadelphia, Univ. of Pennsylvania, 1935, pp. 1-21.

130. ——: "The skull of Swift," *Bookman* [New York], 66 (Jan. 1928), 503-8.

131. ——: *The skull of Swift,* London, Chatto & Windus, 1929; also Indianapolis, Bobbs-Merrill, 1928. See A. E. Case, *SRL,* 4 (Apr. 7, 1928), 739-40; D. MacCarthy, *Life and letters,* 1 (July 1928), 136-40; G. Sampson, *Bookman* [London], 74 (July 1928), 197-99; *TLS,* Sept. 27, 1928, p. 682.

132. ——: "Swift and Stella," *Landmark,* 12 (May 1930), 286-90.

133. ——: "The Swift apocrypha," *Life and letters,* 1 (Aug. 1928), 237. See D. MacCarthy, *ibid.,* pp. 237-38.

134. ——: "Swift's handwriting" [MS. of Temple's *Memoirs*], *TLS,* July 24, 1930, p. 611.

135. Longe, Julia G., ed.: *Martha Lady Giffard, her life and correspondence (1664-1722),* London, Allen, 1911.

136. Longford, [Edward Arthur Henry Pakenham, 6th] Earl of: *Yahoo; a tragedy in three acts,* Dublin, Hodges & Figgis [1934]. Reprinted in *Plays of changing Ireland,* ed. by C. Canfield, New York, Macmillan, 1936, pp. 153-91.

137. Ludwig, W.: *Lord Bolingbroke und die Aufklärung,* Heidelberg, C. Winter, 1928.

138. Macy, John: "Swift's relations with women," *New republic,* 28 (Nov. 16, 1921), 354-55. Reprinted in *The critical game,* New York, Boni & Liveright, 1922, pp. 163-72. Review of 553.

139. *Manch, Joseph: "Jonathan Swift and women," *Univ. of Buffalo Studies,* 16 (Monographs in English, no. 3), 1941, pp. 135-214. See D. Cornu, *MLQ,* 2 (June 1941), 328-29.

140. Marburg, Clara: *Sir William Temple: a seventeenth century "libertin,"* New Haven, Yale U.P., 1932.

141. Maxwell, Constantia: *Dublin under the Georges, 1714-1830,* London, Harrap, 1936.

142. Meynell, Alice: "Mrs. Dingley," in *Essays* [1914], London, Burns, Oates, 1930; also New York, Scribner, 1914, pp. 201-6.

143. Mundy, P. D.: "Dryden and Swift: their relationship," *N&Q,* 147 (Oct. 4, 18, Nov. 8, 1924), 243-44, 279-80, 334.

143a. Myers, Elizabeth: *The basilisk of St. James,* London, Chapman & Hall, 1945. [Fiction].

144. Nergard, Ebbe: "Forholdet mellem Swift og Stella," *Edda, Nordisk Tidskrift,* 27 (1927), 46-74.

145. Newman, Bertram: *Jonathan Swift,* London, Allen & Unwin, 1937; also Boston, Houghton, 1937. See *TLS,* June 5, 1938, p. 425; and 51.

146. Nicol, J. C.: *Swift and Stella,* Farnham, Langham, 1926.

147. *The Orrery papers,* ed. by the Countess of Cork and Orrery, London, Duckworth, 1903, 2v.

148. Petitjean, A[rmand] M.: "L'Enfance de Swift," *Mesures,* 4 (Jan. 1938), 67-79.

149. ——: "Swift et Stella," *Cahiers du sud,* 24 (Dec. 1937), 720-33.

150. Piper, A. Cecil: "Swift's Stella" [baptismal entry], *N&Q,* 184 (May 22, 1943), 323. See H. Williams, *ibid.* (June 5, 1943), 351.

151. Reed, Myrtle: *Love affairs of literary men,* New York, Putnam, 1907, pp. 3-18.

152. Reid, Eva Charlotte: "Manifestations of manic-depressive insanity in literary genius," *American journal of insanity,* 68 (Apr. 1912), 595-632. See 110.

153. Rice, J. A., Jr.: "A letter from Stella" [to Capt. Dingley], *TLS,* May 29, 1930, p. 457. See H. Williams, *ibid.,* June 5, 1930, p. 478; S. Leslie, *ibid.,* July 24, 1930, p. 611.

154. Roch, H.: "Swift und Stella," *Kölnische Zeitung,* 1939, no. 278.

155. Rossi, M. Manlio: "Essay on the character of Swift" [trans. by J. M. Hone], *Life and letters,* 8 (Sept. 1932), 342-57.

156. —— and J. M. Hone: *Swift; or, the egotist,* London, Gollancz, 1934; also New York, Dutton, 1934. See F. T. Wood, *ESt,* 69 (1934), 119-20; M. Praz, *English studies,* 17 (1934), 228-31; and 63.

157. [Schnittkind, Henry Thomas, and D. A.:] "Jonathan Swift," in *Living biographies of famous novelists,* by Henry Thomas and Dana Lee Thomas, New York, Garden city, 1943, pp. 63-76.

158. *Scott, Temple, ed.: *The prose works of Jonathan Swift* . . . with a biographical introduction by W. E. H. Lecky, London, Bell, 1897-1908; reprinted, 1900-14, 12v.

159. ——: "Two portraits of Swift" [queries on Jervas and Bindon], *Athenaeum*, 110, no. 3637 (July 10, 1897), 73. See W. Roberts, *ibid.*, no. 3638 (July 17, 1897), 105; S. Lane-Poole, *ibid.*, no. 3640 (July 31, 1897), 169; and 81.

160. Sharp, Robert F.: "Swift the man," in *Architects of English literature*, New York, Dutton, 1900, pp. 54-66.

161. Sheppard, Alfred Tresidder: "Swift and Stella," *Bookman* [London], 73 (March 1928), 311-13.

162. Sherburn, George: *The early career of Alexander Pope*, New York, Oxford U.P., 1936.

163. Sichel, Walter: *Bolingbroke and his times*, London, Nisbet, 1901-2, 2v.

164. Sitwell, Edith: *I live under a black sun*, London, Gollancz, 1939. [Fiction].

165. Smith, Sophie Shilleto: *Dean Swift*, London, Methuen [1910]; also New York, Putnam, 1910.

166. Stephen, Leslie: *Jonathan Swift* [1882], London, Macmillan, 1931.

167. ——: "Jonathan Swift," in *Dictionary of national biography*, 55 (1898), 204-27.

168. Strahan, J. A.: "Swift and Ireland," *Blackwood's magazine*, 208 (Aug. 1920), 210-24.

169. ——: "Swift, Steele, and Addison," *Blackwood's magazine*, 208 (Oct. 1920), 493-510.

170. Straus, Ralph: *Robert Dodsley, poet, publisher and playwright*, London and New York, Lane, 1910.

171. ——: *The unspeakable Curll*, London, Chapman & Hall, 1927.

172. Strout, Alan Lang: "Scott and Swift" [editorial problems; Swift as a collector], *TLS*, Apr. 21, 1932, p. 291.

173. *Sutherland, James R.: "Dr. Swift in London," in *Background for Queen Anne*, London, Methuen, 1939, pp. 78-123.

174. Thomas, Edward: *Feminine influence on the poets*, London, Secker, 1910; also New York, Lane, 1911.

175. *Thomas, Joseph M.: "Swift and the stamp act of 1712," *PMLA*, 31 (June 1916), 247-63.

176. Thomas, Paul Karl: *Die literarische Verkörperung der philantropischen Zuges in der englischen Aufklärung*, Münsterberg, 1929. (Breslau diss.).

177. Van Doorn, Cornelis: *An investigation into the character of Jonathan Swift,* Amsterdam, Swets and Zeitlinger, 1931. See W. A. Eddy, *PQ,* 11 (Apr. 1932), 208-9; H. Williams, *RES,* 8 (July 1932), 347-49; P. Meissner, *Anglia Beiblatt,* 44 (Jan. 1933), 13-16.

`178. Van Doren, Carl.: "Conjured spirit," *SRL,* 7 (Sept. 13, 1930), 117-19. Reprinted in 179.

179. ——: *Swift,* New York, Viking, 1930. See *TLS,* Apr. 30, 1931, p. 343; and 203.

180. Walters, J. Cuming: "Jonathan Swift, man and idealist," *Manchester quarterly,* 40 (Jan. 1921), 1-19.

181. Warrick, John: "The spiritual Quixote," *TLS,* Apr. 7, 1927, p. 251.

182. *Williams, Harold: *Dean Swift's library, with a facsimile of the original sale catalogue* [1745], *and some account of two manuscript lists of his books,* Cambridge, Cambridge U.P., 1932. See *TLS,* Aug. 4, 1932, p. 555; H. C. Hutchins, *RES,* 9 (Oct. 1933), 488-94; and 50; 115; 124; 125; 211.

183. ——: "Stella's friends" [poem in T. Sheridan's handwriting], *TLS,* May 9, 1936, p. 400.

184. ——: "Swift's Stella," *N&Q,* 184 (Apr. 10, 1943), 223. Comment on 112.

185. Wilson, T. G.: "Swift's deafness; and his last illness," *Irish journal of medical science,* 6th ser., no. 162 (June 1939), 241-56. Reprinted in *Annals of medical history,* 3rd ser., 2 (July 1940), 291-305. See 56.

186. Winchester, Caleb Thomas: "Life of Jonathan Swift," in *Old castle and other essays,* New York, Macmillan, 1922, pp. 181-236.

187. Wolffersdorf-Leslie, A. Von: "Was Swift married to Stella," *Anglia,* 18 (1896), 1-55.

188. Woodbridge, Homer E.: *Sir William Temple,* New York, Modern Language Association, 1940.

189. Woods, Margaret L.: "Swift, Stella, and Vanessa," *Nineteenth century,* 74 (Dec. 1913), 1230-47. Reprinted in *Transactions of the Royal society of literature,* 2nd-ser., 32 (1914), 185-214.

190. Yeats, William Butler: "The words upon the window pane," in *Wheels and butterflies,* London, Macmillan, 1934, pp. 5-63. Reprinted in *Plays of changing Ireland,* ed. by C. Canfield, New York, Macmillan, 1936, pp. 11-24. [Drama].

See also: 250, 320, 453, 550, 553, 555, 568.

III. GENERAL CRITICISM

191. Aitken, George A.: "Swift," in *Cambridge history of English literature.* Cambridge, Cambridge U.P., and New York, Putnam, 1912, v. 9, pp. 91-128. Reprinted, Cambridge, Cambridge U.P., and New York, Macmillan, 1933.

192. Bailey, John Cann: "Swift," in *Studies in some famous letters,* London, 1899.

193. Baker, Ernest A.: *The history of the English novel,* London, Witherby, 1929, v. 3, pp. 230-50.

194. Baker, Harry T.: "Jonathan Swift," *Sewanee review,* 34 (Jan.-Mar. 1926), 1-11.

195. Barbosa, Ruy: "Ensaio sobre Swift," in *Orações do Apostolo,* Rio de Janeiro, 1923, pp. 147-250.

196. Barnett, John Egger: "The posthumous reputation of Dean Swift," in *Harvard university. Graduate school of arts and sciences. Summaries of theses . . . 1938,* Cambridge, Harvard U.P., 1940, pp. 286-89.

197. Becker, Hans Philipp Otto. *Die Satire Jonathan Swifts,* Halle, Karras, 1913. (Marburg diss.).

198. Beckingham, C. F.: "Johnson on Swift and Fuller on De Dominis," *N&Q,* 169 (Oct. 19, 1935), 276.

199. *Berwick, Donald M.: *The reputation of Jonathan Swift, 1781-1882,* Philadelphia, 1941. (Princeton diss.).

200. Boyd, Ernest: "A new way with old masterpieces: Jonathan Swift," *Harper's magazine,* 150 (Apr. 1925), 584-94. Reprinted as "Jonathan Swift," in *Literary blasphemies,* New York and London, Harper, 1927, pp. 74-105.

201. Chesterton, G. K.: "On Jonathan Swift," in *All I survey,* London, Methuen, 1933, pp. 69-73; also New York, Dodd, 1933, pp. 82-87.

202. Chubb, Edwin Watts: "Swift," in *Masters of English literature,* Chicago, McClurg, 1914, pp. 102-22.

203. Colum, Mary M.: "Jonathan Swift," *SRL,* 7 (Nov. 22, 1930), 357-59. Reprinted in *Designed for reading,* New York, Macmillan, 1934, pp. 303-12. Review of 179.

204. Connolly, Cyril: "Sterne and Swift," *Atlantic monthly,* 175 (June 1945), 94-96.

205. Cordelet, Henriette: *Swift,* Paris [1907].

206. *Davis, Herbert: "The conciseness of Swift," in *Essays on the eighteenth century presented to David Nichol Smith,* ed. by J. R. Sutherland and F. P. Wilson, Oxford, Clarendon, 1945, pp.15-32.

207. *——: "Recent studies of Swift: a survey," *Univ. of Toronto quarterly,* 7 (Jan. 1938), 273-88. Review of 42 recent articles and books.

208. ——: "Swift and the pedants," *Oriel review* [1 (1943),] 129-44.

209. Davis, Kathryn: "A note on the *Spectator 459*" [quotation from Swift, *Thoughts,* 1711], *MLN,* 60 (Apr. 1945), 274.

210. Dennis, John: *The age of Pope* [1894], London, Bell, 1929.

211. Eddy, William A.: "Interpreters of the age of Swift," *SP,* 31 (July 1934), 490-95. Review of 35, 92, 182 and 516.

212. Eisner, Kurt: "Jonathan Swift," *Sozialistische Monatshefte,* 3 (Sept. 1911), 1234-42.

213. Ferrau, Antonio: "Idee di Swift sull'arte politica," *Rivista internazionale di filosofia del diritto,* 14 (1934), 244-56.

214. Frye, Prosser Hall: "Swift, ludibrium rerum humanarum," in *Literary reviews and criticism,* New York and London, Putnam, 1908, pp. 82-103.

215. Gregory, Horace: "On William Butler Yeats and the mask of Jonathan Swift," in *Shield of Achilles; essays on beliefs in poetry,* New York, Harcourt, 1944, pp. 136-55.

216. Gückel, W., and Günther, E.: *Daniel Defoes und Jonathan Swifts Belesenheit und literarische Kritik,* Leipzig, Meyer and Müller, 1925 (*Palaestra* 149). See R. S. Crane, *PQ,* 5 (Oct. 1926), 371.

217. Gwynn, Stephen: "Pope and Swift," in *Masters of English literature,* New York, Macmillan, 1904, pp. 170-99.

218. Hayward, John: "Jonathan Swift," in *From Anne to Victoria,* ed. by Bonamy Dobrée, London, Cassell, 1937; also New York, Scribner, 1937, pp. 29-40.

219. Herrmann, Max: *Attacken von Jonathan Swift,* München, 1919.

220. Irazusta, Julio: "Swift, escritor," *Nosotros,* 3 (1938), 346-47.

221. Kacziány, Géza: *Swift Es Kora,* Budapest, Eggenberger-Féle Könyvkereskedes, 1901.

222. Knight, G. Wilson: "Swift and the symbolism of irony," in *The burning oracle,* London, Oxford U.P., 1939, pp. 114-30.

223. *Korn, Max Armin: *Die Weltanschauung Jonathan Swifts,* Jena, Biedermann, 1935. See E. Pons, *JEGP,* 36 (Apr. 1937), 288-89; R. Quintana, *MLN,* 52 (Apr. 1937), 298-302.

224. Kronenberger, Louis: "Artists," in *Kings and desperate men,* New York, Knopf, 1942, pp. 131-58.

225. *Landa, Louis A.: "Swift's economic views and mercantilism," *ELH,* 10 (Dec. 1943), 310-35.

226. *Leavis, F. R.: "The irony of Swift," *Scrutiny,* 2 (Mar. 1934), 364-78. Reprinted in *Determinations,* London, Chatto, 1934, pp. 79-108.

227. Lerner, Max: "Jonathan Swift: literary anthropologist," in *Ideas are weapons; the history and uses of ideas,* New York, Viking, 1939, pp. 293-96.

228. Leslie, Shane: "Jonathan Swift," *Outlook* [London], 60 (Oct. 8, 1927), 481-82.

229. Looten, C[amille]: *La pensée religieuse de Swift et ses antinomies,* Lille, Facultés catholiques, 1935 (Mémoires et travaux, fasc. 45). See E. Pons, *RAA,* 13 (Feb. 1936), 243-45; *TLS,* Mar. 21, 1936, p. 248; L. A. Landa, *MP,* 34 (Aug. 1936), 86-88.

230. Lynd, Robert: "The politics of Swift and Shakespeare," in *The art of letters,* New York, Scribner, 1921, pp. 139-49.

231. McCarthy, Justin: *The reign of Queen Anne,* New York and London, Harper, 1902, v. 1, pp. 222-44.

232. *McKenzie, Gordon: "Swift: reason and some of its consequences," in *Five studies in literature* (Univ. of California Publications in English, v. 8, no. 1), Berkeley, 1940, pp. 101-29.

233. Martini, Esther: *Jonathan Swift,* Rimini, Garattoni, 1933.

234. Massingham, H. W.: "Shaw and Swift," in *Modern English essays,* ed. by E. Rhys, London, Dent, and New York, Dutton, 1922, v. 4, pp. 103-10.

235. Mauthner, Fritz: *Der Atheismus und seine Geschichte im Abendlande,* Stuttgart-Berlin, Deutsche Verlags-Anstalt, 1921, v. 2, pp. 553-64.

236. Maxwell, J. C.: "Demigods & pickpockets: the augustan myth in Swift and Rousseau," *Scrutiny,* 11 (Summer 1942), 34-39.

236a. "The melancholy of Swift," *TLS,* Oct. 20, 1945, p. 498. Review of 109a; 374; 474.

237. More, Paul Elmer: "Dean Swift," *Nation,* 101 (Aug. 5, 1915), 171-73. Reprinted in *Shelburne essays,* Boston, Houghton, 1919, v. 10, pp. 101-21. Review of 550.

238. Moriarty, Gerald P.: *Dean Swift and his writings,* London, Seeley, 1893.

[33]

239. Nevinson, Henry Woodd: " 'Where cruel rage'," in *Essays in freedom and rebellion*, New Haven, Yale U.P., 1921, pp. 67-74.

240. "New light on Swift," *TLS*, Jan. 10, 1935, pp. 13-14. Review of 393; 568.

241. *O'Conor, Charles: "George Faulkner and Jonathan Swift," *Studies*, 24 (Sept. 1935), 473-86.

242. O'Leary, R. D.: "Swift and Whitman as exponents of human nature," *International journal of ethics*, 24 (Jan. 1914), 183-201.

243. Page, T. E.: "Jonathan Swift," *Bookman* [London], 53 (Nov. 1917), 55-58. Review of 275.

244. Paul, Herbert: "Prince of journalists," *Nineteenth century*, 47 (Jan. 1900), 73-87. Reprinted in *Men and letters*, London, Lane, 1901, pp. 261-83.

245. Petitjean, A[rmand]: *Présentation de Swift: études et larges extraits*, Paris, Gallimard, 1939.

246. Pons, Emile: "Fielding, Swift et Cervantes (de 'Don Quixote in England' à 'Joseph Andrews')," *Studia-neophilologica* [Uppsala], 15, no. 3 (1943).

247. *Potter, George R.: "Swift and natural science," *PQ*, 20 (Jan. 1941), 97-118. See L. A. Landa, *PQ*, 21 (Apr. 1942), 219-21.

248. Powers, William H.: "Swift and Mark Twain," *Nation*, 93 (Sept. 21, 1911), 262.

249. Powys, Llewellyn: "Jonathan Swift," *Freeman*, 6 (Nov. 1, 1922), 177-79.

250. *Quintana, Ricardo: *The mind and art of Jonathan Swift*, London and New York, Oxford U.P., 1936. See *TLS*, Jan. 2, 1937, p. 9; H. Davis, *PQ*, 16 (Apr. 1937), 187-88; H. Williams, *RES*, 13 (Apr. 1937), 235-38; L. A. Landa, *MP*, 35 (Nov. 1937), 202-4; E. Pons, *MLN*, 53 (May 1938), 389-91; and 207; 261.

251. ——: "Recent discussions of Swift," *College English*, 2 (Oct. 1940), 11-18.

252. Randi, A. Lo Forte: *Nelle letterature straniere, pessimisti*, Palermo, Seeber, 1902.

253. "Ranger": "Jonathan Swift," *Bookman* [London], 30 (June 1906), 96-97.

254. Read, Herbert: "Two notes on Swift" [1. Poetry; 2. Life of reason], in *In defence of Shelley*, London, Heinemann [1936], pp. 165-82.

255. Rébora, Piero: *Jonathan Swift*, Rome, Formiggini, 1922; also London, Truslove & Hanson, 1922.

[34]

256. Rolleston, T. W.: "Two makers of modern Ireland" [Berkeley and Swift], *Fortnightly review*, 91 (June 1909), 1100-16.

257. *Ross, John F.: *Swift and Defoe: a study in relationship*, Berkeley, Univ. of California, 1941. See L. A. Landa, *PQ*, 21 (Apr. 1942), 221-23; W. D. Taylor, *RES*, 19 (Jan. 1943), 89-90; A. W. Secord, *MLN*, 58 (Dec. 1943), 642. See 269.

258. Scudder, Vida D.: *Social ideals in English letters*, Boston, Houghton, 1923, pp. 89-113.

259. Seccombe, Thomas: "Jonathan Swift," *Bookman* [London], 32 (Sept. 1907), 193-96.

260. Sewald, Josef: *Swifts Entwicklung zum Satiriker*, Augsburg, Schroff, 1933. (Munich diss.).

261. *Sherburn, George: "Methods in books about Swift," *SP*, 35 (Oct. 1938), 635-56.

262. Skelton, Sir John: "An apology for the dean," in *Summers and winters at Balmawhapple: a second series of table-talk of Shirley* Edinburgh and London, 1896, v. 2, pp. 217-54.

263. *Smith, David Nichol: "Jonathan Swift: some observations," in *Essays by divers hands. Transactions of the Royal society of literature*, 14 (1935), 29-48.

264. Squire, J. C.: "The utopian satirist," in *Life and letters*, London, Hodder [1920], pp. 125-31; also New York, Doran [1921], pp. 137-44.

265. Stephen, Leslie: *English thought in the eighteenth century*, 4th ed., New York, Putnam [1927], 2v.

265a. Sutherland, James R.: "Some aspects of eighteenth century prose," in *Essays on the eighteenth century presented to David Nichol Smith*, ed. by J. R. Sutherland and F. P. Wilson, Oxford, Clarendon, 1945, pp. 94-110.

266. Taylor, Coley B.: *Mark Twain's margins on Thackeray's Swift*, New York, Gotham house, 1935.

267. *Taylor, W. D.: *Jonathan Swift, a critical essay*, London, Davies, 1933. See H. Williams, *RES*, 10 (Oct. 1934), 477-80; and 63.

268. Tucker, W. J.: "Irish masters of prose" [Swift, Goldsmith, Burke], *Catholic world*, 144 (Mar. 1937), 712-17.

269. Van Maanen, W.: "Defoe and Swift," *English studies*, 3 (June 1921), 65-69. See 257.

270. Wagenknecht, E. C.: "Swift as fictionist," in *Cavalcade of the English novel*, New York, Holt, 1943, pp. 42-45.

271. *Watkins, W. B. C.: " 'Absent thee from felicity'," *Southern review,* 5 (1939), 346-65. Reprinted in 272.
272. ——: *Perilous balance. The tragic genius of Swift, Johnson & Sterne,* Princeton, Princeton U.P., 1939.
273. Webster, Clarence M.: "Swift and the English and Irish theatre" [and Gay], *N&Q,* 163 (Dec. 24, 1932), 452-54.
274. Westgate, R. I. W., and MacKendrick, Paul L.: "Juvenal and Swift," *Classical journal,* 37 (May 1942), 468-82.
275. Whibley, Charles: *Jonathan Swift,* Cambridge, Cambridge U.P., 1917. Reprinted in *Literary studies,* London, Macmillan, 1919, pp. 343-70. See 243.
276. Willey, Basil: " 'Nature' in satire," in *The eighteenth century background,* New York, Columbia U.P., 1941, pp. 95-109.
277. Wyld, Henry Cecil: *A history of modern colloquial English,* London, Unwin [1920]; 3rd ed., Oxford, Blackwell, 1936.

See also: 34, 60, 79, 145, 179.

IV. FOREIGN REPUTATION AND INFLUENCE

278. Aigner, G. V. Klem: *Rabeners Verhältnis zu Swift,* Pola, 1905.
279. Cooke, Alice L.: "Some evidence of Hawthorne's indebtedness to Swift," *Univ. of Texas Studies in English,* no. 18 (1938), 140-62.
280. Faguet, Emile: "Voltaire, son education, littéraire," *Revus des cours et conférence,* viii[2] (1900), 289-96.
281. Gates, Floy Perkinson: "James Otis and Jonathan Swift," *New England quarterly,* 5 (Apr. 1932), 344-46.
282. *Goulding, Sybil: *Swift en France,* Paris, Champion, 1924. See F. Baldensperger, *RLC,* 4 (Oct.-Dec. 1924), 702-4; E. Pons, *RAA,* 2 (Apr. 1925), 348-50; and 293; 295.
283. Haber, Tom Burns: "Gulliver's travels in America" [Lulbegrud creek, Kentucky], *American speech,* 11 (Feb. 1936), 99-100.
284. Kruuse, Jens: "Holberg og Swift," in *Fem danske Studier tilegnet Vilh. Andersen,* Copenhagen, Branner, 1934, pp. 48-67.
285. Müller, Willi: *The Monikins von J. F. Cooper in ihrem Verhältnis zu Gulliver's travels von J. Swift,* Rostock, Hinstorff, 1900.
286. Pechel, Rudolf: "Der Feind der Yahoos. Zum 150. Jubiläum der ersten deutschen Uebersetzung von Gullivers Reisen," *Deutsche Rundschau,* 256 (July 1938), 36-40.

287. Philippović, Vera: *Swift in Deutschland,* Agram, Dionićka Tiskara u Zagrebu, 1903. (Zürich diss.)

288. Pienaar, William J. B.: *English influences in Dutch literature and Justus van Effen as intermediary,* Cambridge, Cambridge U.P., 1929.

289. Price, Mary Bell, and Price, Lawrence Marsden: *The publication of English literature in Germany in the 18th century,* Berkeley, Univ. of California, 1934, pp. 231-33.

290. Ross, John F.: "Character of Poor Richard: its source and alteration," *PMLA,* 55 (Sept. 1940), 785-94.

291. Stephens, Kate: "Was Benjamin Franklin a plagiarist? Poor Richard's almanac and Isaac Bickerstaff," *Bookman,* 4 (Sept. 1896), 24-30. See 290.

292. Streeter, Harold Wade: *The eighteenth century English novel in French translation: a bibliographical study,* New York, Institute of French studies [1936], pp. 52-59.

293. Thibaudet, Albert: "Swift in France," *London mercury,* 11 (Mar. 1925), 532-34. Review of 282.

294. Walden, Helen: *Jean Paul and Swift,* New York, 1940. (New York Univ. diss.).

295. Webster, Clarence M.: "Omissions from *Swift en France,*" *MLN,* 47 (Mar. 1932), 152-53. Addenda to 282.

296. ——: "Washington Irving as an imitator of Swift" [*The history of New York* and *Gulliver*], *N&Q,* 166 (Apr. 28, 1934), 295.

V. THE BATTLE OF THE BOOKS

297. *Burlingame, Anne Elizabeth: *The battle of the books in its historical setting,* New York, Huebsch, 1920. See J. W. Bright, *MLN,* 36 (Dec. 1921), 508-12; and 302.

298. Diede, Otto: *Der Streit der Alten und Modernen in der englischen Literaturgeschichte des XVI. und XVII. Jahrhunderts,* Greifswald, Adler, 1912.

299. Garrod, H. W.: "Phalaris and Phalarism," in *Seventeenth century studies presented to Sir Herbert Grierson,* Oxford, Clarendon, 1938, pp. 360-71.

300. Gillot, Hubert: *La Querelle des anciens et des modernes en France,* Paris, Champion, 1914.

301. Guthkelch, A. C., ed.: *The battle of the books; with selections from the literature of the Phalaris controversy*, London, Chatto, 1908.

302. *Jones, Richard Foster: *Ancients and moderns, a study of the background of the battle of the books* (Washington Univ. Studies, n.s., Language and literature, no. 6), St. Louis, 1936. See M. E. Prior, *MP,* 34 (Feb. 1937), 322-26; C. S. Northup, *JEGP,* 36 (Apr. 1937), 278-81; R. W. Frantz, *MLN,* 52 (June 1937), 447-49; M. Praz, *English studies,* 20 (June 1938), 130-35.

303. *——: "The background of the *Battle of the books,*" *Washington Univ. studies 7, Humanistic series 2* (1920), 99-162.

304. Mac Cain, John W.: "Swift and Heywood" [*Battle of the books* and *Spider and the flie*], *N&Q,* 168 (Apr. 6, 1935), 236-38.

305. Morrison, Felix: "A note on *The battle of the books,*" *PQ,* 13 (Jan. 1934), 16-20.

306. "Notes on Swift" [*Contests and dissensions* and *Battle of the books*], *N&Q,* 160 (May 16, 1931), 350.

307. Seeger, Oskar: *Die Auseinandersetzung zwischen Antike und Moderne in England bis zum Tode Dr. S. Johnsons,* Berlin and Leipzig, 1927.

308. Webster, Clarence M.: "Two Swift imitations" [of *Battle of the books* and *Tale of a tub*], *MLN,* 51 (Nov. 1936), 441.

See also: 111, 312, 316, 374, 393.

VI. A TALE OF A TUB

309. Baughan, Denver Ewing: "Swift and Gentillet," *SP,* 37 (Jan. 1940), 64-74.

310. Boyce, Benjamin: "Predecessors of 'The tale of a tub'," *N&Q,* 168 (Feb. 16, 1935), 110-11. Reply to 327.

311. Dargan, H. M.: "The nature of allegory as used by Swift" [particularly in *Tale of a tub* and *Gulliver*], *SP,* 13 (July 1916), 159-79.

312. *Davis, Herbert, ed.: *A tale of a tub with other early works 1696-1707,* Oxford, Blackwell, 1939. (*Prose works,* v. 1). See H. Williams, *RES,* 15 (July 1939), 356-58; P. Meissner, *ESt,* 73 (1939), 401-3.

313. de Castro, J. Paul: "Swift: the groaning elm-board," *N&Q,* 180 (Mar. 8, 1941), 170.

314. *Guthkelch, A. C.: "Swift's 'Tale of a tub'," *MLR*, 8 (July 1913), 301-13; (Oct. 1913), 454-63; 9 (Jan. 1914), 100; 10 (Apr. 1915), 181-87.

315. ——: " 'The tale of a tub revers'd' and 'Characters and criticisms upon the ancient and modern orators,' etc.," *Library*, 3rd ser., 4 (July 1913), 270-84. Reprinted, London, Morning, 1913.

316. *——and Smith, D. N., eds.: *A tale of a tub to which is added The battle of the books and the Mechanical operation of the spirit*, Oxford, Clarendon, 1920.

317. Heller, Bernhard: "Zur Geschichte der Parabel vom echten Ringe," *Zeitschrift für vergleichende Litteraturgeschichte*, 16 (1906), 479-85.

318. Hofmann, Hermann: *Swift's Tale of a tub*, Leipzig-Reudnitz, A. Hofmann, 1911.

319. Legouis, Pierre: "Marwell et Swift. Note sur un passage du *Conte du tonneau*," *RAA*, 1 (Feb. 1924), 240-42.

320. *Pons, Emile: *Swift: les années de jeunesse et le 'Conte du tonneau,'* (Publications de la faculté des lettres de l'Université de Strasbourg, fasc. 26), Strasbourg, 1925. See H. Williams, *RES*, 1 (Oct. 1925), 487-92; R. S. Crane, *MP*, 23 (Nov. 1925), 232-33; L. Cazamian, *RAA*, 3 (Oct. 1925), 68-70; P. Dottin, *Revue de l'enseignement des langues vivantes*, 42 (1925), 361-62; and 471; 540.

321. Scott, Temple, ed.: *A tale of a tub and other early works.* (V. 1 of *Prose works;* see 158).

322. Webster, Clarence M.: "A possible source for *A tale of a tub*" [a 1613 German romance], *MLN*, 48 (Apr. 1933), 251-53.

323. ——: "The Puritan's ears in *A tale of a tub*," *MLN*, 47 (Feb. 1932), 96-97.

324. *——: "The satiric background of the attack on the Puritans in Swift's *A tale of a tub*," *PMLA*, 50 (Mar. 1935), 210-23.

325. *——: "Swift and some earlier satirists of Puritan enthusiasm," *PMLA*, 48 (Dec. 1933), 1141-53.

326. ——: "Swift's *Tale of a tub* compared with earlier satires of the Puritans," *PMLA*, 47 (Mar. 1932), 171-78.

327. ——: "Tom Brown and *The tale of a tub*," *TLS*, Feb. 18, 1932, p. 112. See E. K. Linton, *ibid.*, Feb. 25, 1932, p. 134; and 310.

328. Williams, Harold: "Swift's 'Tale of a tub'," *TLS*, Sept. 30, 1926, p. 654.

See also: 111, 300, 308, 374, 393, 471, 507, 508.

329. Baumgartner, Ira P.: *Swift's Drapier's letters,* Ithaca, 1934. (Abstract of Cornell diss.).
330. Davies, Godfrey: "A new edition [1749] of Swift's *The story of the injured lady,*" *HLQ,* 8 (Aug. 1945), 388-92.
331. *——: "Swift's *The Story of the injured lady,*" *HLQ,* 6 (Aug. 1943), 473-89.
332. *Davis, Herbert, ed: *The drapier's letters and other works, 1724-1725,* Oxford, Blackwell, 1941. (*Prose works,* v. 10). See H. Williams, *RES,* 18 (July 1942), 354-56.
333. *——: *The drapier's letters to the people of Ireland against receiving Wood's halfpence,* Oxford, Clarendon, 1935. See *TLS,* May 30, 1935, p. 345; M. J. McManus, *Dublin magazine,* 10 (July-Sept. 1935), 71-72; E. Pons, *Etudes Anglaises,* 1 (Jan. 1936), 71-72; M. A. Korn, *Anglia Beiblatt,* 47 (Jan. 1936), 75-78; L. A. Landa, *Univ. of Toronto quarterly,* 5 (Jan. 1936), 295-99; H. Williams, *TLS,* June 6, 1935, p. 364, and *RES,* 12 (July 1936), 355-59; R. Quintana, *MLN,ᵗ* 52 (Apr. 1937), 298-302.
334. G., F.: "A pamphlet by Swift" [*The present miserable state of Ireland*], *Athenaeum,* 107, no. 3567 (Mar. 7, 1896), 314.
335. Glaser, Hans: *Jonathan Swifts Kritik an der englischen Irlandpolitik,* Ohlau i. Schl., Eschenhagen [1932]. (Breslau diss.). See M. A. Korn, *Anglia Beiblatt,* 47 (Jan. 1936), 75-78.
336. *Goodwin, A.: "Wood's halfpence," *English historical review,* 51 (Oct. 1936), 647-74.
337. Hone, Joseph M.: "Berkeley and Swift as national economists," *Studies,* 23 (Sept. 1934), 421-32.
338. *Landa, Louis A.: "*A modest proposal* and populousness," *MP,* 40 (Nov. 1942), 161-70. See 343.
339. *Rothschild, Lord: "The publication of the first Drapier letter," *Library,* 4th ser., 19 (June 1938), 107-15.
340. Scott, Temple, ed.: *The drapier's letters.* (V. 6 of *Prose works;* see 158).
341. ——: *Historical and political tracts—Irish.* (V. 7 of *Prose works*).
342. Stockley, W. F. P.: "Swift as an Irish writer," *Irish ecclesiastical record,* ser. 5, 27 (Feb. 1926), 127-47.

343. *Wittkowsky, George. "Swift's *Modest proposal*: the biography of an early Georgian pamphlet," *JHI*, 4 (Jan. 1943), 74-104. See L. A. Landa, *PQ*, 23 (Apr. 1944), 178-79; and 338.

See also: 25, 141, 168, 225, 256, 474.

VIII. GULLIVER'S TRAVELS

344. Aitken, G. A.: "Coleridge on 'Gulliver's travels' " [MS. criticism], *Athenaeum*, 108, no. 3590 (Aug. 15, 1896), 224.

345. Allinson, Francis G.: *Lucian, satirist and critic*, Boston, Marshall, Jones, 1926.

346. Atkinson, Geoffroy: *The extraordinary voyage in French literature before 1700*, New York, Columbia U.P., 1920.

347. ———: *The extraordinary voyage in French literature from 1700 to 1720*, Paris, Champion, 1922.

348. ———: *Les relations de voyages du XVII siècle et l'evolution des idees*, Paris, Champion [1924].

349. Ault, Norman: "Pope and Gulliver," *National review*, 122 (June 1944), 510-16.

350. Baughan, Denver Ewing: "Swift's source of the Houyhnhnms reconsidered," *ELH*, 5 (Sept. 1938), 207-10. See rejoinder by R. W. Frantz, *ibid.*, 6 (Mar. 1939), 82.

351. Bennett, James O'Donnell: "Swift's 'Gulliver's travels'," in *Much loved books*, New York, Boni and Liveright, 1927, pp. 333-38.

352. Bennett, R. E.: "A note on the Cyrano-Swift criticism," *MLN*, 43 (Feb. 1928), 96-97. Comment on 372.

353. Bernbaum, Ernest, ed.: *Gulliver's travels*, New York, Harcourt [1920].

354. Birrell, Augustine: "Gulliver's travels," in *Collected essays and addresses, 1880-1920*, London and Toronto, Dent, 1922, v. 1, pp. 94-99.

355. Bonner, Willard Hallam: *Captain William Dampier, buccaneer-author*, Stanford, Stanford U.P., 1934.

356. *Bracher, Frederick: "The maps in *Gulliver's travels*," *HLQ*, 8 (Nov. 1944), 59-74. See 359; 415.

357. Brown, Arthur C. L.: "Gulliver's travels and an Irish folk-tale," *MLN*, 19 (Feb. 1904), 45-46. See 388; 410.

[41]

358. Brown, Huntington: *Rabelais in English literature*, Cambridge, Harvard U.P., 1933.

359. *Case, Arthur E.: *Four essays on Gulliver's travels* [text; geography; satire; significance], Princeton, Princeton U.P., 1945.

360. *——ed.: *Gulliver's travels*, New York, Nelson, 1938.

361. Child, Harold: "Some English utopias," *Transactions of the Royal society of literature*, n.s., 12 (1933), 31-60.

362. *Clubb, Merrel D.: "The criticism of Gulliver's 'Voyage to the Houyhnhnms,' 1726-1914," in *Stanford studies in language and literature*, ed. by Hardin Craig, Stanford, Stanford U.P., 1941, pp. 203-32.

363. Darnall, F. M.: "Old wine in new bottles," *South Atlantic quarterly*, 41 (Jan. 1942), 53-63.

364. *Davis, Herbert, ed.: *Gulliver's travels, 1726. With an intro. by Harold Williams*, Oxford, Blackwell, 1941. (*Prose works*, v. 11). See W. D. Taylor, *RES*, 18 (July 1942), 356-58.

365. *Dege, Charlotte: *Utopie und Satire in Swifts Gulliver's travels*, Frankfort (Oder), Trowitzsch, 1934. (Jena diss.).

366. Dennis, G. R., ed.: *Gulliver's travels*. (V. 8 of *Prose works*, ed. by T. Scott; see 158).

367. Digeon, Aurélien: " 'Gulliver' et La Bruyère," *RAA*, 3 (Feb. 1926), 245-47.

368. Dobrin, Milton B.: "Lilliput revisited: Reynolds, Fronde, dimensional analysis, and Dean Swift," *Technology review*, 47 (1945), 299-300, 320-26.

369. Duncan, Carson S.: *The new science and English literature in the classical period*, Menasha, Wis., Banta, 1913.

370. Eddy, William A.: "*The anatomist dissected*—by Lemuel Gulliver," *MLN*, 41 (May 1926), 330-31.

371. ——: "Cyrano de Bergerac and *Gulliver's travels*," *MLN*, 38 (June 1923), 344-45.

372. *——: *Gulliver's travels, a critical study*, Princeton, Princeton U.P., 1923. See E. Pons, *RLC*, 4 (Jan.-Mar. 1924), 149-54; A. W. Secord, *JEGP*, 23 (July 1924), 460-62; and 352; 359; 362; 364; 386; 387; 388; 409; 412; 416; 419; 421; 422; 437; 441.

373. ——: "*Gulliver's travels* and *Le théâtre italien*," *MLN*, 44 (June 1929), 356-61.

374. —— ed.: *Gulliver's travels, A tale of a tub, Battle of the books, etc.*, New York, Oxford U.P., 1933. See 236a.

375. ——: "Ned Ward and 'Lilliput'," *N&Q*, 158 (Mar. 1, 1930), 148-49.

376. Eddy, William A.: "Rabelais—a source for *Gulliver's travels*," *MLN*, 37 (Nov. 1922), 416-18.

377. ——: "A source for Gulliver's first voyage" [Lucian's *Icaromennipus*], *MLN*, 37 (June 1922), 353-55.

378. ——: "A source for *Gulliver's travels*" [D'Ablancourt's Sequel to Lucian's *True history*], *MLN*, 36 (Nov. 1921), 419-22.

379. *Elder, Lucius W.: "The pride of the Yahoo," *MLN*, 35 (Apr. 1920), 206-11.

380. Ferenczi, S.: "Gulliver-Phantasien," *Internationale Zeitschrift für Psychoanalyse*, 13 (1927), 379-96.

381. *Firth, Sir Charles H.: "The political significance of Gulliver's travels," *Proceedings of the British academy*, 9 (1919-20), 237-59. Reprinted in *Essays, historical and literary*, Oxford, 1938, pp. 210-41.

382. ——: "A story from *Gulliver's travels*," *RES*, 2 (July 1926), 340-41.

383. *Frantz, R. W.: "Gulliver's 'Cousin Sympson'," *HLQ*, 1 (Apr. 1938), 329-34.

384. *——: "Swift's Yahoos and the voyagers," *MP*, 29 (Aug. 1931), 49-57.

385. Gould, S. H.: "Gulliver and the moons of Mars," *JHI*, 6 (Jan. 1945), 91-101.

386. Gove, Philip Babcock: "Gildon's 'Fortune shipwreck' as background for *Gulliver's travels*," *RES*, 18 (Oct. 1942), 470-78.

387. ——: *The imaginary voyage in prose fiction . . . with an annotated check list of 215 imaginary voyages from 1700 to 1800*, New York, Columbia U.P., 1941.

388. Grennan, Margaret R.: "Lilliput and Leprecan: Gulliver and the Irish tradition," *ELH*, 12 (Sept. 1945), 188-202. See 357; 410.

389. "Gulliver's travels (October 28, 1726)," *TLS*, Oct. 28, 1926, pp. 729-30.

390. Handro, Lilli: *Swift, Gulliver's travels: eine Interpretation im Zusammenhang mit den geistesgeschichtlichen Beziehungen*, Hamburg, Friederichsen, 1936.

391. Hanford, James H.: "Plutarch and Dean Swift," *MLN*, 25 (June 1910), 181-84.

392. Hartmann, C. Hughes: *Gulliver in Lilliput . . . put into basic*, London, K. Paul, 1934.

393. Hayward, John, ed.: *Gulliver's travels* [1735 text] *and selected writings in prose and verse*, London, Nonesuch, and New York, Random house, 1934. See 240.

394. Heidler, Joseph B.: *The history, from 1700 to 1800, of English criticism of prose fiction* (Univ. of Illinois Studies in language and literature, 13), Urbana, 1928.

395. Herrman, Louis: *In the sealed cave, being a modern commentary on a strange discovery made by Captain Lemuel Gulliver in the year 1721*, London, Williams and Norgate [1935]. [Fiction].

396. Horrell, Joe: "What Gulliver knew," *Sewanee review*, 51 (Oct. 1943), 476-504.

397. Hubbard, Lucius L.: *Notes on the adventures and surprizing deliverances of James Dubourdieu and his wife: A source for Gulliver's travels; Also the adventures of Alexander Vendchurch, London, 1719*, Ann Arbor, Ann Arbor press, 1927.

398. Hübener, Gustav: "Die Entstehung von *Gulliver's travels* und die 'curiosity'-Kultur," *Neophilologus,* 7 (1922), 35-57.

399. James, M. R.: "Swift's copy of Dampier," *TLS,* Feb. 26, 1925, p. 138.

400. Karpman, Ben.: "Neurotic traits of Jonathan Swift, as revealed in *Gulliver's travels,*" *Psychoanalytic review,* 29 (1942), 26-45, 165-84.

401. Kaufman, P.: "Literary centenaries of 1926," *Bookman* [New York], 62 (Jan. 1926), 572-75.

401a. Kliger, Samuel: "The unity of Gulliver's travels," *MLQ,* 6 (Dec. 1945), 401-15.

402. Lachèvre, Frédéric: *Les Successeurs de Cyrano de Bergerac,* Paris, Champion, 1922.

403. Lahontan, Louis Armand, Baron de: *Dialogues curieux entre l'auteur et un sauvage de bons sens qui a voyagé,* ed. by Gilbert Chinard, Baltimore, Johns Hopkins press, 1931.

404. Lauchert, Friedrich: "Die pseudo-swiftische Reise nach Kaklogallinien [S. Brunt] und in den Mond in der deutschen literatur," *Euphorion Zeitschrift für literaturgeschichte,* 18 (1911), 94-98, 478.

405. Lawton, H. W.: "Bishop Godwin's *Man in the moone,*" *RES,* 7 (Jan. 1931), 23-55.

406. Leslie, Shane, intro.: *The travels of Lemuel Gulliver,* New York, Limited editions club, 1929.

407. Lewis, Penry: "Lilliput and Gulliver," *N&Q,* 12th ser., 4 (Mar. 1918), 73. See E. Bensly, *ibid.* (May 1918), 140.

408. McCracken, George: "Homerica in *Gulliver's travels,*" *Classical journal,* 29 (Apr. 1934), 535-38.

409. McCue, G. S.: "A seventeenth century Gulliver" [*The weekly comedy,* 1699], *MLN,* 50 (Jan, 1935), 32-34. See 441.

410. Mezger, F.: "Swifts 'Gullivers travels' und irische Sagen," *Archiv für das Studium der neueren Sprachen und Literaturen,* 151 (Oct. 1926), 12-18. See 357; 388.

411. Montagu, M. F. Ashley: *Edward Tyson, 1650-1708,* Philadelphia, American philosophical society, 1943.

412. ——: "Tyson's Orang-outang, sive Homo Sylvestris and Swift's *Gulliver's travels,*" *PMLA,* 59 (Mar. 1944), 84-89.

413. *Moore, John Brooks: "The rôle of Gulliver," *MP,* 25 (May 1928), 469-80.

414. Moore, John Robert: "A Defoe allusion in 'Gulliver's travels'," *N&Q,* 178 (Feb. 3, 1940), 79-80.

415. *——: "The geography of *Gulliver's travels,*" *JEGP,* 40 (Apr. 1941), 214-28. See 356; 359.

416. ——: "A new source for *Gulliver's travels*" [Tyssot de Patot: *Voyages ... de Jacques Masse,* 1710], *SP,* 38 (Jan. 1941), 66-80.

417. Morley, Henry, ed.: *Gulliver's travels and other works. Exactly reprinted from the first edition ... with some account of Cyrano de Bergerac and of his voyages to the sun and moon,* London, Routledge, 1906.

418. Mudie, Sidney A.: "A misplaced paragraph in 'Gulliver's travels'," *TLS,* June 30, 1927, p. 460. See H. Williams, *ibid.,* July 28, 1927, p. 520; and 449.

419. Nicolson, Marjorie: "The microscope and English imagination," *Smith College Studies in modern languages,* 16, no. 4, Northampton, 1935. See 247; 369.

420. ——ed.: *A voyage to Cacklogallinia ... by Samuel Brunt,* New York, Facsimile text society, 1940.

421. *—— and Mohler, Nora M.: "The scientific background of Swift's Voyage to Laputa," *Annals of science,* 2 (1937), 299-334.

422. *——: "Swift's 'flying island' in the Voyage to Laputa," *Annals of science,* 2 (1937), 405-30.

423. Nock, S. A.: "Gulliver and Yahoos," *SRL,* 9 (Sept. 17, 1932), 113. Reply to W. H. Bonner, "Yes a Yahoo," *ibid.* (Aug. 6, 1932), p. 34.

424. ——: "Not a Yahoo," *SRL,* 8 (July 16, 1932), 846.

425. Papini, Giovanni: "Jonathan Swift," in *Stroncature,* 4th ed., Firenze, Libreria della voce [1919], pp. 319-28. Reprinted in *Four and twenty minds,* New York, Crowell, 1922, pp. 219-27.

[45]

426. Paso, Antonio, y Joaquin Abati: *Los viajes de Gulliver; zarzuela cómica en tres actos,* Madrid, Velasco, 1911.

427. Patterson, Richard F.: "Two emendations" [fardels, not saddles, in Voyage to Laputa, ch. 5] *TLS,* Aug. 29, 1936, p. 700.

428. Phelps, William Lyon: "A note on Gulliver," *Yale review,* 17 (Oct. 1927), 92-98.

429. Poll, Max: *The sources of Gulliver's travels* (Univ. of Cincinnati Bulletin no. 24; Publications of the university, ser. 2,. v. 3). Cincinnati [1904]. See 372.

430. Pons, Emile, ed.: *Gulliver's travels: extraits,* Paris, Hachette, 1927.

431. *——: "Rabelais et Swift à propos du Lilliputien," in *Mélanges offerts à M. Abel Lefranc,* Paris, Droz, 1936, pp. 219-28.

432. ——: "Le voyage genre littéraire au XVIIIe siècle," *Bulletin de la faculté des lettres de l'université de Strasbourg,* 4 (1926), 97-101, 144-49, 201-7.

433. Read, Herbert: "Swift," in *The sense of glory,* Cambridge, Cambridge U.P., 1930; also New York, Harcourt, 1930, pp. 80-99. Reprinted in *Collected essays in literary criticism,* London, Faber, 1938, pp. 196-219.

434. Reed, Edward Bliss: *"Gulliver's travels* and Tom Brown" *MLN,* 33 (Jan. 1918), 57-58. See 501.

435. Robertson, M. E. I.: "Dean Swift and modern methods" [Gulliver's method of learning languages], *Modern languages,* 8 (Dec. 1926), 44-46.

436. Roch, H.: "Swifts Gulliver," *Stuttgarter Neues Tagblatt,* 1939, no. 386.

437. Rockwell, Frederick S.: "A probable source for 'Gulliver's travels' " [*The humours of a coffee house,* 1699], *N&Q,* 169 (Aug. 24, 1935), 131-33.

438. *Ross, John F.: "The final comedy of Lemuel Gulliver," in *Studies in the comic* (Univ. of California Publications in English, v. 8, no. 2), Berkeley, 1941, pp. 175-96.

439. Rovillain, Eugène E.: "Jonathan Swift's *A voyage to Lilliput* and *The thousand and one quarters of an hour, Tartarian tales* of Thomas Simon Gueulette," *MLN,* 44 (June 1929), 362-64.

440. Scott, Edward J. L.: "Swift and Lemuel Gulliver" [of Westminster], *Athenaeum,* 126, no. 4074 (Nov. 25, 1905), 725. See G. Aitken and L. R. M. Strachan, *ibid.,* no. 4077 (Dec. 16, 1905), 837-38; and H. Lavers-Smith, *ibid.,* no. 4079 (Dec. 30, 1905), 897-98.

441. Secord, A. W.: "Gulliver and Dampier," *MLN,* 51 (Mar. 1936), 159. Comment on 409.

442. "Swift and Gulliver," *Saturday review,* 128 (Nov. 8, 1919), 435-36. Reprinted in *Living age,* 303 (Dec. 27, 1919), 784-86.

443. Thierkopf, Paul: *Swifts Gulliver und seine französischen Vorgänger,* Magdeburg, Baensch, 1899. (Jahresbericht über die Guericke-Schule).

444. Toldo, Pietro: "Les voyages merveilleux de Cyrano de Bergerac et de Swift et leurs rapports avec l'oeuvre de Rabelais," *Revue des études Rabelaisiennes,* 4 (1906), 295-334; 5 (1907), 24-44.

445. [Van Doren, Mark:] "Two hundred years of Gulliver," *Nation* [New York], 122 (Mar. 17, 1926), 274.

446. Webster, Clarence M.: "Notes on the Yahoos," *MLN,* 47 (Nov. 1932), 451-54.

447. *Wedel, T. O.: "On the philosophical background of *Gulliver's travels,*" *SP,* 23 (Oct. 1926), 434-50. See F. B. Kaye, *PQ,* 6 (Apr. 1927), 190-91.

448. Whibley, Charles: "Gulliver's travels," *Blackwood's magazine,* 220 (Oct. 1926), 549-60.

449. *Williams, Harold, intro.: *Gulliver's travels,* London, First edition club, 1926. See *TLS,* Feb. 10, 1927, p. 88; H. C. Hutchins, *RES,* 3 (Oct. 1927), 466-73; E. Pons, *RAA,* 5 (Dec. 1927), 158-60; and 15.

450. ——: "A sentence of 'Gulliver's travels' in Swift's hand," *TLS,* Jan. 10, 1929, p. 28.

451. Winterich, John T.: "Gulliver's travels," *Publisher's weekly,* 116 (Aug. 17, 1929), 625-29. Reprinted in *Twenty-three books and the stories behind them,* Philadelphia, Lippincott, 1938, pp. 211-18.

See also: 7, 12, 13, 15, 30, 32, 57, 77, 193, 197, 199, 200, 247, 250, 270, 283, 285, 286, 296, 311, 541.

IX. POLITICAL WRITINGS

452. Allen Robert J.: "Swift's earliest political tract [*Contests and dissensions*] and Sir William Temple's essays," in *Harvard studies and notes in philology and literature,* 19 (1937), 3-12.

453. Ball, F. Elrington: "Swift and Prince Butler" [in *Public spirit of the Whigs*], *N&Q,* 12th ser., 7 (Nov. 20, 1920), 404-5.

454. Belloc, Hilaire: "On Jonathan Swift" [and *Public spirit of the Whigs*], *New Statesman*, 33 (Sept. 14, 1929), 681. Reprinted in *A conversation with a cat*, New York, Harper, 1931, pp. 129-34

455. Blanchard, Rae, ed.: *Tracts and pamphlets by Richard Steele*, Baltimore, Johns Hopkins Press, 1944.

456. *Davis, Herbert, ed.: *The Examiner, and other pieces written in 1710-11*, Oxford, Blackwell, 1940. (*Prose works*, v. 3).

457. ——: "Jonathan Swift and the *Four last years of the queen*," *Library*, 4th ser., 16 (Dec. 1935), 344-46. See 468.

458. Harrison, G. B.: "Jonathan Swift," in *Social and political ideas of some English thinkers of the augustan age*, ed. by F. J. C. Hearnshaw, London, Harrap, 1928, pp. 189-209.

459. Holst, Edward D.: "Swift's politics," in *Univ. of Wisconsin summaries of doctoral dissertations*, 7 (1942), 288-90.

460. Laprade, William Thomas: *Public opinion and politics in eighteenth century England*, New York, Macmillan, 1936.

461. Meye, Rudolf: *Die politische Stellung Jonathan Swifts*, Leipzig, Glausch, 1903.

462. Scott, Temple, ed.: *Contributions to "The Tatler," "The Examiner," "The Spectator," and "The Intelligencer."* (V. 9 of *Prose works;* see 158).

463. ——: *Historical and political tracts—English.* (V. 5 of *Prose works*).

464. ——: *Historical writings.* (V. 10 of *Prose works*).

465. Steevens, David H.: *Party politics and English journalism*, Chicago, 1916. (Chicago diss.).

466. Teerink, H.: *The history of John Bull*, Amsterdam, H. J. Paris, 1925. See E. Pons, *RAA*, 4 (Apr. 1927), 354-56; H. M. Dargan, *MLN*, 43 (Feb. 1928), 132-33; and 16; 41.

467. Wheeler, C. B., ed.: *The conduct of the allies*, Oxford, Clarendon, 1916.

468. *Williams, Harold: "Jonathan Swift and the *Four last years of the queen*," *Library*, 4th ser., 16 (June, Dec. 1935), 61-90, 343-44. See 457.

469. ——: "Old Mr. Lewis" [*History of the four last years*], *RES*, 21 (Jan. 1945), 56-57.

See also: 11, 17, 37, 52, 82, 96, 137, 163, 213, 230, 231, 335, 393.

X. MISCELLANEOUS PROSE

470. Bradley, L. J. H.: "Swift's 'Directions to servants'" [and 1738 *Advice to servants*], *TLS*, Feb. 11, 1926, p. 99.

471. Darnall, F. M.: "Swift's religion," *JEGP*, 30 (July 1931), 379-82. Comment on 320.

472. *Davis, Herbert, ed.: *Bickerstaff papers and pamphlets on the church*, Oxford, Blackwell, 1939. (*Prose works*, v. 2).

473. Eddy, William A. "Tom Brown and Partridge the astrologer," *MP*, 28 (Nov. 1930), 163-68.

474. ——ed.: *Satires and personal writings*, London and New York, Oxford U.P., 1932. See 236a.

475. *——: "The wits vs. John Partridge, astrologer," *SP*, 29 (Jan. 1932), 29-40.

476. Flasdieck, Hermann M.: *Der Gedanke einer englischen Sprach-Akademie in Vergangenheit und Gegenwart*, Jena, Frommann-schen, 1928.

477. Foley, Louis: "Three sermons on the Trinity," *American church monthly* (June 1928), 302-313. Reprinted, with slight changes, as "A triptych of the Trinity," *Holy cross magazine* (Aug. 1942), 236ff.

478. Gimblett, C.: "The great dean and the young preacher," *London quarterly and Holborn review*, 170 (Apr. 1945), 160-62.

479. Graham, Walter: *English literary periodicals*, New York, Nelson, 1930.

480. Hand, George, ed.: *Two rare pamphlets* [*Mr. Baron L—'s charge* and *A hue and cry after Dr. Swift*] *attributed to Swift* (California State Library, Sutro branch, Occasional papers, reprint series, no. 4), San Francisco, 1939.

481. Hazard, Paul: "Comment les enfants se sont emparés de Swift," *Les Nouvelles littéraires*, 10 (Sept. 12, 1931), 8.

482. Hornbeak, Katherine: "Swift's 'Letter to a very young Lady'," *HLQ*, 7 (Feb. 1944), 183-86.

483. Huxley, Aldous: "Polite conversation," in *On the margin*, London, Chatto, 1923, pp. 87-93.

484. "Jonathan Swift, 1667-1745, Einwände gegen die Abschaffung des Christentums," *Deutsche Rundschau*, 246 (Feb. 1936), 108-12.

485. Krappe, Edith S.: "A 'lapsus calami' of Jonathan Swift" [in *Letter . . . to a young poet*], *MLN*, 53 (Feb. 1938), 116-17.

486. *Landa, Louis A.: "Swift, the mysteries and deism," *Studies in English, Department of English, Univ. of Texas, 1944,* Austin, 1945, pp. 239-56.

487. Linn, Irving: "Dean Swift, Pope Innocent, and Oliver Wendell Holmes" [*Meditation on a broomstick*], *PQ,* 16 (July 1937), 317-20. See 500.

488. Matthews, Albert: "The Iroquois virtuosi" [in *Mechanical operation*], *N&Q,* 176 (June 10, 1939), 410-11.

489. Neumann, J. H.: "Jonathan Swift and English pronunciation," *Quarterly journal of speech,* 28 (Apr. 1942), 198-201.

490. ———: "Jonathan Swift and English spelling," *SP,* 41 (Jan. 1944), 79-85.

491. ———: "Jonathan Swift and the vocabulary of English," *MLQ,* 4 (June 1943), 191-204.

492. Reimers, Hans: *Jonathan Swift: Gedanken und Schriften über Religion und Kirche,* Hamburg, Friederichsen, de Gruyter, 1934. See M. A. Korn, *Anglia Beiblatt,* 46 (May 1935), 149-55; W. Graham, *JEGP,* 34 (Oct. 1935), 601-3; H. Williams, *RES,* 12 (Jan. 1936), 97-100.

493. Roderick, P.: "L'Astrologue mort et vivant; une mystification au XVIIIᵉ siècle," *Mercure de France,* 286 (Aug. 15, 1938), 73-80.

494. Rühl, Ernst: "Grobianus in England," *Palaestra,* 38 Berlin, 1904.

495. Saintsbury, George: "Swift" [and *Polite conversation*], in *Prefaces and essays,* London, Macmillan, 1933, pp. 1-11.

496. Schevill, Rudolph: "Swift's hoax on Partridge, the astrologer, and similar jests in fiction," *Connecticut Academy of arts and sciences, Transactions,* 15 (July 1909), 227-38.

497. Scott, Temple, ed.: *Literary essays.* (V. 11 of *Prose works;* see 158).

498. ———: *Writings on religion and the church.* (V. 3-4 of *Prose works*).

499. Secord, A. W.: "Did Swift write the 'Memoirs' " [of Captain Carleton], in *Studies in the narrative method of Defoe,* Urbana, Univ. of Illinois, 1924, pp. 204-6. See A. Parnell, "Dean Swift and *The memoirs of Captain Carleton,*" *English historical review,* 6 (Jan. 1891), 97-151.

500. Smith, Grace P.: "Rabelais and the figure of man as inverted tree," *PQ,* 17 (Apr. 1938), 218-19. Comment on 487.

501. Thompson, Elbert N. S.: "Tom Brown and eighteenth century satirists," *MLN,* 32 (Feb. 1917), 90-94. See 434.

502. Thompson, Paul V.: "Swift and the Wagstaffe papers," *N&Q*, 175 (July 30, 1938), 79.

503. Trench, W. F., and Garratt, K. B.: "John Macky's Memoirs with Swift's notes," *TLS*, Aug. 13, 20, 1938, pp. 536, 548.

504. ——: "On Swift's marginalia in copies of Macky's *Memoirs*," *Library*, 4th ser., 19 (Dec. 1938), 354-62.

505. Van Lennep, William: "Three unnoticed writings of Swift" [*Directions to players; The toper;* and a 1735 letter to Mrs. Pendarves], *PMLA*, 51 (Sept. 1936), 793-802.

506. Webster, Clarence M.: "A source for Swift's *Meditation upon a broom-stick*" [Gascoigne], *MLN*, 51 (Mar. 1936), 160.

507. ——: "Swift and the Royal society's 'Philosophical transactions' " [the meaning of "hamated"], *N&Q*, 161 (Aug. 8, 1931), 99-100. See *idem.* (Sept. 12, 1931), 194.

508. ——: "Temple [*Treatise concerning enthusiasm*], Casaubon and Swift," *N&Q*, 160 (June 6, 1931), 405.

509. Wilson, Mona: "Swift's Polite conversation," *English*, 1 (1936), 150-55.

See also: 37, 103, 108, 113, 117, 229, 235, 265, 290, 291, 316, 335, 393, 456, 462, 463, 464.

XI. POETRY

510. Aitken, G. A.: "Jonathan Swift" [and the seven penny papers on Dunkirk], *Athenaeum*, no. 3850 (Aug. 10, 1901), 189-90.

511. Allhusen, E. L.: "A Swift epitaph?" [on Bishop Burnet; not by Swift], *TLS*, May 2, 1935, p. 288. See H. Williams, *ibid.*, May 9, 1935, p. 301.

512. Alspach, Russell King: "Molyneux, Swift, and Mac Curtin," in *Irish poetry, from the English invasion to 1798*, Philadelphia, Univ. of Pennsylvania, 1943, pp. 75-80.

513. Ball, F. Elrington: "Swift's verse," *N&Q*, 12th ser., 8 (Jan. 1, 1921), 1-3. See *idem.*, 12 (Mar. 3, 1923), 174; and 2.

514. *——: *Swift's verse, an essay*, London, Murray [1929]. See *N&Q*, 156 (Feb. 16, 1929), 125-26; E. Pons, *RAA*, 7 (Apr. 1930), 343-45; and 531.

515. Bensly, Edward: "Swift: 'An ass's hoof' " [in *On burning a dull poem*], *N&Q*, 168 (Mar. 23, 1935), 210.

516. Bond, Richmond P.: *English burlesque poetry 1700-1750,* Cambridge, Harvard U.P., 1932. See 211.

517. Breslar, M. L. R.: "Lines on Swift" [affixed to St. Patrick's in 1713; attributed to Smedley], *N&Q,* 9th ser., 6 (Aug. 11, 1900), 107. See George Marshall, *ibid.* (Sept. 1, 1900), 177-78; John Pickford, *ibid.* (Oct. 13, 1900), 292.

518. Brooks, E. St. John: "A poem of Swift's" [variant of *On the little house . . . Castleknock*], *TLS,* July 10, 1943, p. 331.

519. Browning, W. E., ed.: *Poems,* London, Bell, 1910, 2v. Replaced by 543; see 538.

520. Case, Arthur E.: "Philips or Carey," *TLS,* May 22, 1930, p.434. See 535; 545.

521. Davis, Herbert: "The poetry of Jonathan Swift," *College English,* 2 (Nov. 1940), 102-15. Review of 543.

522. *——: "Swift's view of poetry," in *Studies in English by members of University college, Toronto,* Toronto, Univ. of Toronto, 1931, pp. 9-58.

523. *——: "Verses on the death of Dr. Swift," *Book-collectors' quarterly,* 2 (Mar.-May 1931), 57-73.

524. Doughty, Oswald: *English lyric in the age of reason,* London, O'Connor, 1922, pp. 67-71.

525. Esdaile, Katherine A.: "The fairy feast," *TLS,* Feb. 12, 1931, p. 116. See H. Williams, *ibid.,* Feb. 19, 1931, p. 135.

526. Fairchild, H. N.: "Indifference, negation, scepticism," in *Religious trends in English poetry,* New York, Columbia U.P., 1939, v. 1, pp. 3-40.

527. Gulick, Sidney Lewis, Jr.: "Jonathan Swift's 'The day of judgment'," *PMLA,* 48 (Sept. 1933), 850-55.

528. Harper, Charles G. H.: "Swift's visits to England: the 'Four crosses' inn" [and window verse in 1730], *N&Q,* 9th ser., 9 (Mar. 8, 1902), 186-87. See J. T. Page, *ibid.* (Apr. 19, 1902), 312.

529. McGovern, J. B.: "Two epitaphs by Dean Swift," *N&Q,* 156 (June 22, 1929), 442. See reply by V. B. Neuburg, *ibid.,* 157 (July 13, 1929), 32.

530. Matthes, Heinrich: "Die Verschleierung der Verfasserschaft bei englischen Dichtungen des 18. Jahrhunderts," *Beiträge zur Erforschung der Sprache und Kultur Englands und Nordamerikas,* 4 (1928), 33-112.

531. "The poems of Swift," *TLS,* July 4, 1929, pp. 521-22. Review of 514; 532.

532. Roberts R. Ellis, ed.: *Miscellaneous poems by Jonathan Swift,* [Waltham St. Lawrence], Golden cockerell press, 1928. See 531.

533. ——: "Swift in his poems and minor writings," in *Readings for pleasure and other essays,* London, Methuen, 1928, pp. 197-222.

534. Segar, Mary: "Ambrose Philips," *TLS,* Dec. 7, 1933, p. 875.

535. ——: "Philips or Carey," *TLS,* Apr. 3, 24, 1930, pp. 298, 352. See 520; 545.

536. Shuster, George N.: "Ode writers of the augustan age," in *The English ode from Milton to Keats,* New York, Columbia U.P., 1940, pp. 146-85.

537. Suddard, S. J. Mary: "Swift's poetry," in *Keats, Shelley, and Shakespeare,* Cambridge, Cambridge U.P., 1912, pp. 231-51.

538. "Swift's poems," *Living age,* 266 (Sept. 10, 1910), 670-75. Review of 519.

539. Thompson, Paul Vern: "Verses on Blenheim" [1714], *TLS,* Aug. 22, 1936, p. 680.

540. Webster, Clarence M.: *"Hudibras* and Swift" [*Baucis and Philemon*], *MLN,* 47 (Apr. 1932), 245-46. Comment on 320.

541. ——: "The Yahoo's overthrow," *TLS,* May 14, 1931, p. 390.

542. Williams, Harold: "A hue and cry after dismal," *RES,* 6 (Apr. 1930), 195-96.

543. *—— ed.: *The poems of Jonathan Swift,* Oxford, Clarendon, 1937, 3v. See *TLS,* Aug, 21, 1937, pp. 597-98; R. K. Root, *PQ,* 17 (Apr. 1938), 206-7; E. Pons, *Etudes Anglaises,* 2 (Oct. 1938), 404-7; R. Quintana, *MLN,* 54 (Jan. 1939), 59-61; H. Davis, *MP,* 35 (Feb. 1938), 335-38; Lord Rothschild, *Cambridge review,* 59 (1939), 147-48; and 521.

544. —— and Lord Rothschild. *"The grand question debated,"* *RES,* 15 (July 1939), 328-30.

545. Wood, Frederick T.: "Philips or Carey" [as object of satire in *A Christmas box for Namby-Pamby*], *TLS,* Feb. 27, Apr. 10, May 8, pp. 166, 318, 394. See 520; 535.

546. Wyld, Henry Cecil: *Studies in English rhymes from Surrey to Pope,* London, Murray, 1923.

See also: 1, 3, 4, 9, 18, 22, 23, 29, 33, 72, 254, 393, 474, 494.

547. Aitken, George A., ed.: *The journal to Stella,* London, Methuen, 1901.
548. ——: "Swift's 'Journal to Stella'," *Critic,* 39 (Sept. 1901), 235-39.
549. Ardagh, J.: "Queries from Swift's 'Journal to Stella' " [places and contemporary prices], *N&Q,* 169 (Aug. 24, 1935), 140. See 556.
550. *Ball, F. Elrington, ed.: *The correspondence of Jonathan Swift,* London, Bell, 1910-14, 6v. See 237.
551. *Dearing, Vinton A.: "New light on the first printing of the letters of Pope and Swift," *Library,* 4th ser., 24 (June-Sept. 1943), 74-80. See 561.
552. de Castro, J. Paul: "Addison and Swift" [as letter writers], *N&Q,* 181 (Sept. 13, 1941), 149.
553. *Freeman, A. M.: *Vanessa and her corespondence with Swift,* London, Selwyn and Blount, 1921. See A. Brandl, *Archiv,* 142 (Dec. 1921), 259-60; and 138.
554. Hill, George Birkbeck, ed.: "Some unpublished letters," *Atlantic monthly,* 80 (Aug., Sept., Nov., Dec. 1897), 157-70, 343-54, 674-85, 784-96. Reprinted in 555.
555. ——: *Unpublished letters of Dean Swift,* London, Unwin, 1899.
556. Hocking, W. O. T.: "Queries from Swift's 'Journal to Stella'," *N&Q,* 169 (Aug. 10, 1935), 99. Reply to 549.
557. Irvine, L. L.: "Swift," in *Ten letter-writers,* London, L. &. V. Woolf, 1932, pp. 181-201.
558. Johnson, R. B., ed.: *Eighteenth century letters,* New York, Holt, 1898, 2v. (V. 1 contains letters by Swift, with intro. by S. Lane-Poole).
559. Lane-Poole, Stanley: "Swift's correspondence," *Quarterly review,* 218 (Jan. 1913), 49-70.
560. Leslie, Shane: "Lost letters of Swift," *SRL,* 11 (Feb. 16, 1935), 496. Review of 568.
561. *Mack, Maynard: "The first printing of the letters of Pope and Swift," *Library,* 4th ser., 19 (Mar. 1939), 465-85. See 551.
562. *Moorhead, J. K., ed.: *Swift's Journal to Stella,* London and Toronto, Dent, and New York, Dutton [1924].
563. Parker, Philip: "Swift's letters," *Bookman* [London], 79 (Nov. 1930), 150-52.
564. Pearl, Raymond: "Dean Swift and the goldfish" [shorthand in the letters], *American speech,* 1 (Mar. 1926), 315-16.

565. *Pons, Emile: "Du nouveau sur le 'Journal à Stella'," *Etudes Anglaises*, 1 (May 1937), 210-29.

566. Roberts, W.: "Letters of Pope [to Fortescue] and Swift" [to Ford], *Athenaeum*, 107, no. 3577 (May 16, 1896), 650-51. See 568.

567. Ryland, Frederick, ed.: *The journal to Stella.* (V. 2 of *Prose works*, ed. by Temple Scott; see 158). Reprinted, separately, London, Bell, 1923.

568. *Smith, David Nichol, ed.: *The letters of Jonathan Swift to Charles Ford*, Oxford, Clarendon, 1935. See *TLS*, Jan. 10, 1935, pp. 13-14; H. Williams, *RES*, 11 (Oct. 1935), 489-94; M. Praz, *English studies*, 17 (1935), 228-31; L. A. Landa, *U. of Toronto quarterly*, 5 (Jan. 1936), 295-99; J. R. Sutherland, *MLR*, 31 (July 1936), 431-33; R. Quintana, *MLN*, 52 (Apr. 1937), 298-302; and 560.

569. Strachey, Lytton: "Pope, Addison, Steele, and Swift," in *Characters and commentaries*, London, Chatto, 1933; also New York, Harcourt, 1933, pp. 11-21.

570. "Swift's Journal to Stella," *TLS*, Sept. 24, 1925, pp. 605-6.

571. *Williams, Harold: "Deane Swift, Hawkesworth, and the *Journal to Stella*," in *Essays on the eighteenth century presented to David Nichol Smith*, ed. by J. R. Sutherland and F. P. Wilson, Oxford, Clarendon, 1945, pp. 33-48.

572. ——: "The 'Journal to Stella' " [queries about names], *N&Q*, 184 (Feb. 27, June 5, 1943), 137-38, 376; 187 (Sept. 23, 1944), 147.

573. Woolf, Virginia: "Swift's 'Journal to Stella'," in *The second common reader*, London, L. & V. Woolf, 1932; also New York, Harcourt, 1932, pp. 68-79.

See also: 5, 37, 69, 72, 74, 78, 173, 474, 505.

Index

Index

[*References are to item numbers, not to pages*]

[60]